W9-AGT-106

Independent Africa and the World

By the same author

Nuremberg: the facts, the law and the consequences
Survey of International Affairs 1947 – 48
Survey of International Affairs 1949 – 50
Survey of International Affairs 1951
Survey of International Affairs 1952
Survey of International Affairs 1953
Middle East Crisis (with Guy Wint)
South Africa and World Opinion
World Order and New States
Suez: ten years after (with Anthony Moncrieff)
Total War: Causes and courses of the Second World War (with Guy
    Wint)
World Politics since 1945 (fourth edition, 1982)
The British Experience 1945 – 75
Freedom to Publish (with Ann Bristow)
Top Secret Ultra

INDEPENDENT AFRICA
AND THE WORLD

Peter Calvocoressi

Wingate .... Library

Longman
London and New York

099813

Longman Group Limited

Longman House, Burnt Mill, Harlow
Essex CM20 2JE, England
Associated companies throughout the world

*Published in the United States of America
by Longman Inc,. New York*

© Longman Group Limited 1985

All rights reserved; no part of this publication may be reproduced, stored in a retrieval system, or transmitted in any form or by any means, electronic, mechanical, photocopying, recording, or otherwise, without the prior written permission of the Publishers.

First published 1985

British Library Cataloguing in Publication Data

Calvocoressi, Peter
    Independent Africa and the world.
    1. Africa—Foreign relations—1960-
    I. Title
    327'.096   DT30.5
    ISBN 0-582-29654-4

Library of Congress Cataloging in Publication Data

Calvocoressi, Peter.
    Independent Africa and the world.

    Includes index.
    1. Africa—Politics and government—1960- —Addresses, essays, lectures. 2. Africa—Economic conditions—1960- —Addresses, essays, lectures. 3. Africa—Foreign relations—1960- —Addresses, essays, lectures. 4. Africa—Dependency on foreign countries—Addresses, essays, lectures. I. Title. DT30.5.C34 1985
    960'.32   84 - 875
    ISBN 0-582-29654-4

Set in 10/11pt Linotron 202 Plantin
Printed in Hong Kong by
Wing Lee Printing Co Ltd

CONTENTS

FOREWORD

This book owes its existence to a series of seminars given in the School of Advanced Studies of the Università degli Studi in Florence at the invitation of Professor Antonio Cassese. I am doubly grateful to Professor Cassese who instigated me to prepare the course and, incidentally, to ponder on it afterwards. As a result I have expanded the arguments which I presented to his students – as diverse in their national origins as any I have ever encountered and I now offer its several topics as a contribution, not to the history of Africa on which I am no expert, but to the study of the interaction of Africa with the rest of the world.

The contrast between the high hopes of liberation and the deep disappointments of today have excited disagreeable emotions ranging from depression to derision. For the millions who live in Africa the record is disheartening and poignant. I do not make it my business to censure either white colonialism or black incompetence, although some grounds for censure of both sorts will inevitably be found in the pages which follow. In examining what has occurred over the past quarter century I concentrate on three aspects which seem to me specially important and unresolved. They are: the weakness of government throughout Africa, the economic quandary, and the interests and interventions of outside powers, notably the super-powers.

I have no comprehensive programme for the future and do not believe that anybody else has or can have. I incline to believe that we have had enough of preaching at Africans and dispensing paternalist advice, just as I believe that Africans too frequently overdo the anti-colonialist – and anti-neocolonialist – line of interpretation of Africa's ills. I believe, finally, that things get better only with tedious effort, and the chapters of this book are therefore dedicated to those who think it worth while making this often unrewarded effort.

Peter Calvocoressi
Bath – August 1983

1 LIBERATION

The joy of liberation cannot be measured by anybody who has not experienced it. This is a uniquely thrilling moment in the life of a people when achievement joins hands with expectation, triumph with hope. There is an extraordinary confluence of individual and co-operative exhilaration, personal and communal zest.

The happiest and best productive example in modern European history is the liberation of the Dutch in the sixteenth century. They had many advantages and they made the most of them: a small population inhabiting a manageable area with resources commensurate with the numbers in them; comparatively advanced in education and technical skills; examplars of the bourgeois virtues of industry and thrift; united in language, purpose and religious beliefs; poised to convert tenacity and valour into good business and great art. It is a success story to compare with the escape of the Greek cities from Persian imperialism or the seizure by England's thirteen North American colonies of their own future and fortunes.

The emancipation of Africa from European rule after the Second World War opened similar windows. But they opened on to a far less propitious landscape and within a generation the view has become murky. Some of the spirit of liberation survives. There is an enormous appetite for learning, from literacy programmes to the excitements of new science in agronomy, computer technology and other marvels. Young people who – chiefly in southern Africa – have been carrying guns and using them in deadly earnest welcome earnestly and enthusiastically the opportunity to learn for themselves and work for others. Africa has produced leaders of outstanding intelligence and character. Its natural resources, above and below ground, are impressive, if haphazardly distributed.

But independent Africa is not a success story: quite the contrary. It has become a byword for incompetent government, political instability and economic disasters, dwarfing the goodwill and good efforts which have persisted in the face of bad fortune, bad management and bad luck. The enthusiasms of independence have ·become the struggling reminders of a once dominant mood and if this mood is to be reasserted Africans and non-Africans have to free themselves to survey a sorry record, not with the object of allocating blame but in order to correct mistakes.

Non-Africans made the mistake of imagining that there was not much they needed to do or ought to do about Africa except leave it alone, while still treating marginal bits of it as adjuncts of their own economies. In view of the condition in which they left their colonies, and the superficiality of the thinking they devoted to decolonization and the post-colonial state, this was to say the least a mistake by the colonial powers. The world as a whole rather supposed that Africa was more or less off the map of world affairs. This was another mistake which gradually emerged with a better appreciation of the importance of Africa's minerals (only gold and to a lesser extent diamonds attracted much attention before independence) and its strategic coastlines on the Mediterranean and Red Sea, the Pacific and South Atlantic Oceans.

Africans made the mistake of supposing, or hoping, that they could construct growing and modern (meaning industrialized) economies out of their own efforts and a sufficiency of foreign aid in gifts, loans and commercial concessions. In every respect they were wrong. The pursuit of industrial growth led to neglect of agriculture and to intolerable accumulations of foreign debt. Foreign aid has been disgracefully meagre; the economically advanced states have only very modestly tempered the world's trading and financial systems to the special pleas of the less advanced; and in the 1970s Africa's inevitable economic involvement with the rest of the world laid it open to big rises in the cost of fuels and other imports and to inflation. Africans who, in response to these unwelcome involvements, thought that they might dispense with foreign money and techniques were also wrong, for the burdens of acquiring these things did not do away with their necessity if African economies are not to stagnate or retrogress.

Few took into account the unparalleled growth of the African population. In many parts of the continent production increased after independence in spite of all the difficulties and mistakes, but people multiplied much faster and so the plight of most of them has got worse. In particular countries this decline has been made more or less acute by the way in which the total national income has been distributed. Some have shared misfortune more equitably than others.

Where numbers grow faster than the size of the cake social justice becomes politically significant as well as ethically obtrusive. Inequality is peculiarly damaging to society and the state if it is on the increase when average personal incomes are declining; and consequently the role of government in regulating the economy and apportioning its product, by social and fiscal measures, becomes exceptionally crucial for the maintenance of human happiness, communal goodwill and political stability. Africa, more than anywhere else in the world, has needed governments which are strong in the sense of commanding administrative competence and popular consent. It has not had them, and this is Africa's most crippling burden.

But Africa is different from the rest of the world only at the margins of its experience. It must not be regarded as a case apart. Its inheritance in the post-colonial phase is shabby but many other states are in a like situation. Its populations are growing the fastest in the world but other populations are growing alarmingly fast too. It contains many countries that are poor or very poor indeed but there are equally poor countries outside Africa. It is eyed acquisitively by great powers but no more so than other parts of the world. It is stuffed with racial, ethnic and religious conflicts but not uniquely. On the credit side its good men and women, its assets, its energies and its streaks of optimism are essentially of a kind to be found in every human society. There is nothing at all to be said for any account of modern Africa which transports its virtues or its villainies, its achievements or its shortcomings, outside the field of experience of the modern world.

The problem to which this book essays to contribute is to describe and analyse the general political and economic troubles of Africa within a world context, neither forgetting the rest of the world nor over-stating its impact. The dangers of generalization are too well advertised to require re-statement but their existence is no reason for not running the familiar risks. Africa is both an amalgam of some fifty states and yet also a continent whose history and geography have given these states – or groups of them – important common experiences, attitudes and problems.

Some states are inherently weak because they lack material things, notably food and the capacity to get a good price for what they do produce. States may also be weak because they are discordant and ill organized – because, in other words, they are badly governed. Although we habitually think of bad government as a powerful tyranny, the consequences of weak and incompetent government may be just as bad. No continent illustrates this fact as clearly as Africa and I therefore examine the problem of government before turning to the economic tangles with which governments have to deal. Effective government is a *sine qua non* of economic management whether economic activity is mainly in private hands or nationalized.

These economic problems are partly natural, partly inherited from the colonial past and partly exacerbated since liberation by African mismanagement and by non-African dominance of the world economy upon which Africa's finances depend. Within Africa, as I attempt to show, there have been varying approaches with depressingly similar outcomes. In response economic policies are re-examined, but re-examination amounts to little more than a re-statement of tried arguments in the light of a little more experience, plus repeated complaints about the hard-heartedness of the outside world. A further response, to which I devote a separate but still tentative chapter, is a political reaction to the economic dilemma: the creation of regional associations which attempt to broaden the economic entity without changing political boundaries. (Which is what the EEC was originally designed to do for Western Europe.)

As all these discussions make clear, it is impossible to think about Africa without repeated glances over the shoulder at the rest of the world. In this context African states, whether severally or even in combination, are weak. But they are not therefore insignificant. Parts of Africa are strategically attractive or economically attractive to outside powers, including the two superpowers. To this extent Africans have something to offer, although their bargaining power is constricted and they are peculiarly vulnerable to the hazards of foreign concupiscence.

Two broad propositions may be stated at the outset. First, the terms in which Africa's future is discussed, by Africans and non-Africans, have changed radically within the first post-liberation generation. At liberation the talk was of development and development meant above all industrialization. The key to progress was to imitate the European countries which had stolen a march on the rest of the world with their industrial revolution. But this recipe is now pursued either hesitatingly or not at all. Whether it was a mirage from the start, or became a mirage because conditions turned unpropitious, is a subordinate issue. What is certain is that hopes once centred on industrialization have been dashed and more attention and more money are now being given to the modernization, in some areas the rescue, of agriculture. Furthermore, the very concept of development by whatever route has been obliterated in many African countries by the more urgent need to survive. To talk of development as millions starve is the most frightful refusal to face facts.

Second, the political articulation of post-liberation Africa into fifty independent sovereign states cannot be taken for granted. That the states constituted at independence may continue to survive, let alone prosper, is a highly questionable proposition. So the place to begin is the map.

I

The names given by geographers to the world's continents are as misleading as they are useful. They cause us to think of large land masses distinct from one another and only secondarily subdivided into the several states which exist within each of them. The broad geographical description plays down the political fragmentation of each continent.

This warning, trite though it may seem, is specially necessary in writing about Africa. Until the 1960s the political variety of Africa was obscured by the colonial status of virtually the whole continent. Unlike other continents Africa was not divided into states. Only Liberia, Ethiopia and Egypt were established states, and even the last two antique lands had been under alien rule in living memory. The history of Africa was a subject of widespread ignorance, relieved among experts by knowledge about European missionary and mercantile activities rather than knowledge about Africans themselves. Atlases commonly put Africa on their last pages and on a smaller scale: two marks of comparative insignificance.

Consequently Africa, although sharply defined on the map, was a political blur and Africans were politically indeterminate both in the eyes of non-Africans and to some extent to themselves. They had tribal and religious affinities but not the national definition common to most of the rest of the modern world.

Within a single generation the outward and visible marks were abruptly changed. Between 1957 and 1980 all non-African rule was removed (except from two Spanish towns on the Moroccan coast, two French islands in the Indian Ocean, and Namibia in the southwest of the continent) and Africa became an agglomeration of independent sovereign states, equal in status among themselves and with the states of other continents, members of the United Nations, participants in a multitude of worldwide international agencies and organizations, and directly parts of the less tangible but no less crucial systems which regulate – or fail to regulate – world trading and finance.

In exchanging dependence for sovereignty Africa also exchanged contacts with a very few colonial powers for freedom to enter into relations – diplomatic, economic – with states all over the world. In reverse, it ceased to be Western European private property and became the object of attention, penetration and manipulation by all who saw advantage to be gained there.

The emancipation of Africa created more than fifty new states, far the largest addition ever made to the comity of nations since the consolidation of the nation state. The liquidation of the empires of Western Europe, not much more than a generation after the extinction of the Austrian, Russian and Ottoman empires, complicated the political map of the world to an unprecedented degree. But its consequences have been not merely numerical. Africa has become stamped with new states whose status is universally accepted but whose coherence and competence are often woefully questionable: in some cases a state may look more like a non-state. It follows both that these states are not easy to deal with and also that their governments cannot easily deal with other states. There is a fragility about the new political pattern in Africa which impedes the business of governments and their external relations. There is also huge inequality among the states of Africa which non-Africans have perceived only imperfectly. Preoccupied at first with learning the names and whereabouts and capitals of these new states, outsiders were slow to notice how vastly they differ from one another – to put it crudely, that in world affairs a few matter much more than most.

Africa contains over 30 million square kilometres. The Sahara desert occupies one-third of it. The northern slice of Africa consists almost entirely of huge states, all but one sparsely populated. From the Atlantic coast of Mauritania eastward to Ethiopia and the Red Sea and northward to the Mediterranean a vast area is filled by nine states of over 1 million square kilometres each (two of them exceed 2 million), which leave room in this zone for only two smaller states – Morocco and Tunisia (with a western Saharan state still struggling to be born). All the rest of the continent can show only three such giants: Zaire, Angola and South Africa (without Namibia). The stereotype of the northern state is one of vastness and emptiness which are not repeated further south. On the map they look not only huge but also menacing; but in general they lack the resources – notably human resources – needed to make much of a splash.

Many of these giants have exiguous populations: Libya, much feared by its neighbours, about 2.5 million inhabitants; Mauritania even fewer; Chad and Niger around 4.5 million each and Mali perhaps 7 million. By contrast Nigeria, which is not one of Africa's twelve giants, has a population more than double that of any other African state. Population densities also provide extreme contrasts, ranging from seventy to eighty persons per square kilometre in Nigeria to around 1 per square kilometre in Mauritania, Botswana and Namibia. (See Appendix A for populations and areas.)

Nor does the political map display differences in wealth, current or latent. Gross GNP varies from over $50 billion to under $0.5 billion. Related to population the scale runs from two or three rich countries where the GNP averages out at $2,000 or more per head per year to some twenty countries where the average is $200 or less. Zaire exhibits every kind of extreme. Its natural resources make it potentially one of the richest countries in the world but most Zairois live miserably and die young, and although it is the second largest state in Africa, it has a population density of only ten per square kilometre. By contrast, Libya's giant size, tiny population and oil wealth give it an extravagant national income per head and an even lower population density than Zaire. Examples of statistical anomalies can be multiplied. They serve to emphasize the great diversity of Africa's sovereign states and the ways in which one source of strength may be offset by constraints of a different nature. (For details see Appendix B).

In sum, few of these states are weighty by international standards. Even South Africa and Nigeria, to pick out the more obvious candidates for a world role, have had little impact on world affairs; Zaire none; Egypt only regionally and outside Africa.

II

The chronological pattern of independence has been significant. Africa's new states came into existence neither simultaneously nor over a long time but within a small cluster of years. And in this period a severe crisis – the war in the Belgian Congo (Zaire) – first divided them and then brought them together in a continental organization based on their several sovereignties.

Piecemeal independence destroyed whatever chances there may have been for the integration of several neighbouring territories as a single, perhaps more effective, state. The divisions uncovered by the Congo crisis created antagonistic blocks and a threat of inter-African hostilities. The outcome of these forces was the crystallization in 1963 of a multiple states system overarched by a single international association embracing (in intention) all the sovereign states of the continent. With the foundation of the Organization for African Unity (OAU) Africa followed the example of the other continents, adopted the primacy of the sovereign state in its fortuitous borders, attempted to sanctify these boundaries determined by accident and colonialism, and opted for a diluted internationalism in preference to a pan-African superstate or large regional federations.

This evolution appears inevitable in retrospect. One of its principal consequences has been the proliferation of weak states whose independence is illusory because they cannot, economically or (if the need were to arise) militarily, stand on their own feet. A related consequence has been the chilling descent from the bubbling euphoria of liberation to the cynicism and incompetence which have spread over much of Africa since that bright dawn.

Some of this tribulation was foreseen. Kwame Nkrumah, the first of the new kings in Africa, was – among many other things – a pan-African visionary. He saw that political independence would mean little if it were unaccompanied by economic independence from the former colonial masters; and he saw that this economic independence could not be gained by a plethora of small African states. Faced with Africa's technical and economic backwardness he wanted a united Africa which, by pooling its economic and human resources, might operate independently in a world from which, as Nkrumah well knew, Africa could not opt out.

Pan-Africanism was an old aspiration to which Nkrumah gave a new turn. Its roots were cultural and West African – also in the Caribbean among the descendants of West Africans who had been abducted for the slave trade. It was an assertion of black values against the denigration of the negro race by whites who ascribed the misfortunes of Africans to a supposedly innate inferiority. It was also an assertion of solidarity, the natural recourse of the weak against the strong, and so a powerful ingredient in the anti-colonial crusade which was in consequence a general movement for the emancipation of Africa rather than a series of disjointed movements for the freedom of separate bits of it.

Nkrumah wanted pan-Africanism to persist after liberation because he regarded the grant of independence as only one step along an uncompleted road. He failed for many reasons. When Ghana became independent in 1957 he was out in front and on his own. Guinean independence came a year later and there was a spate of new states in 1960 and the next few years, but all these successive events took the form of the emancipation of an existing entity; there was never a right moment for the creation of an entirely new state, not in West Africa, still less in Africa as a whole. Circumstances too, as well as timetables, were unpropitious. Nkrumah excited envy and distrust, partly because he stole the show when his country became the first of the new states, partly because his policies and his personal style gave offence to staider leaders in other countries (and his own). Nkrumah came to the fore in the Gold Coast in opposition to established leaders of the freedom movement who lacked his fire and his readiness to enlist popular forces instead of manoeuvring a middle class elite – and who lacked too the streak of autocratic ruthlessness which ultimately perverted his rule and destroyed his regime. Nkrumah scared neighbouring African leaders at least as much as he upset the British, and although he prevailed for a few years in his own country Africa on the whole was not to go his way. On these counts he was a non-starter as a post-liberation pan-African leader.

There were in any case still more powerful obstacles. Africa is too big and its basic communications are too poor. Its colonial rulers constructed some roads and railways but they led from the richer areas to the coast and so to Europe, not to other parts of Africa. Pan-Africanism, whatever its emotional strength, lacked all economic underpinning.

What Nkrumah did achieve was something quite different – an opportunist union which he may have seen as a kernel of pan-Africanism, which was prompted by African sympathy, but which turned into an ideological partnership based therefore on a limiting partisanship incompatible with pan-Africanism. This was the Ghana–Guinea union, later extended to embrace Mali. Its mark on the map was ephemeral and without lasting progeny. It did nothing to further pan-Africanism and it gave lesser regional associations a bad name. But it was not the principal determining factor. This occurred in the much broader French colonial empire.

In 1958 de Gaulle demanded of all twelve French colonies in Western and Equatorial Africa a straight answer to a straight question: a choice between membership of a French '*communauté*' in association with France or independence, immediate and complete and unaided. The posing of this question had more influence on the future of Africa than anything done by Nkrumah or Britain.

It was not the question which had been under discussion in Paris and French Africa before de Gaulle returned to power that year as a result of the failures of the Fourth Republic in Indo-China and Algeria. (Indo-China had a profound, if accidental, impact on African affairs by undermining the Fourth Republic and so giving France its new Gaullist style.) Before de Gaulle's return the dominant question had been whether the French colonies should become independent as separate states or in two much larger confederations. In either event the form of association, if any, with France was considered secondary. De Gaulle's initiative reversed these priorities. In Guinea Sekou Toure answered it by choosing independence. Every other colony (with the possible exception of Niger where the referendum was probably cooked) chose the *communauté*. But Guinea's choice proved to be the historic one, not only for Guinea itself but also – as has much less frequently been emphasized – for Africa as a whole.

For the *communauté* was still-born and with it disappeared all prospect of the large state or confederation of states in French West and Equatorial Africa. Guinea's example proved irresistible and within two years all these French colonies had become independent sovereign states, all of them either small or weak or both.

Whether or not de Gaulle intended this outcome in order to divide French Africa and continue to rule its destinies for the benefit of France it is difficult to say. Motives, undisclosed, are difficult to judge except by the fallible method of relating consequences to causes. There were Africans who themselves had reason to prefer fragmentation. To Félix Houphouet-Boigny in Ivory Coast, a comparatively flourishing seaboard colony, it was obvious that his country's fortunes would be ill served by engulfing it in a confederation with territories as destitute as Mali or Upper Volta. Gabon played a similar role in Equatorial Africa. The event, whatever anybody's intentions may have been, was to set a pattern of separate states which was repeated throughout Africa during the 1960s, the decade of multiple independence. Guinea's 'No' to de Gaulle was formative, its union with Ghana an aberration.

That union was extended to Mali (the former French Sudan) by the same mixture of accident and sympathy. Mali was the name chosen for an association of the four territories of Soudan, Senegal, Dahomey and Upper Volta but the two latter changed their minds, leaving Senegal and Soudan in an incompatible embrace which failed to work and finally Soudan on its own – a despised and rejected state which inherited the name of Mali and was rescued from a deprived isolation by Nkrumah and Sekou Toure. The resulting group of three became the expression of more radical attitudes, opposed to the conservatism of men like Houphouet-Boigny, Leopold Senghor in Senegal and the patricians who took over from the British in Nigeria. This ideological cleavage was sharpened by the civil war which broke out in the Congo five days after the abdication of the Belgians on the last day of June 1960.

The war in the Belgian Congo was the next shaping event in the general history of modern Africa after de Gaulle's challenge of 1958. It was compounded of a mutiny in the Congolese army (the Force Publique) which paralysed the newly installed government of Joseph Kasabuvu and Patrice Lumumba; the attempted secession of Katanga (later Shaba) province under Moise Tshombe; the despatch of a United Nations force to preserve order and save life and, less clearly, to prevent the dismemberment of the state; and the removal, arrest and ultimate murder of Lumumba. All these events took place within six months and roused the most intense emotions. They had two major consequences for the political shape of Africa. In the Congo the Katangan secession was defeated, so that Africa's second largest state remained intact and a successful example of resistance to separatism. More generally, the crisis gave rise to the creation of the OAU which overrode and submerged more partial and rival groupings and sanctified the division of the continent into separate sovereign states within their existing inherited frontiers – frontiers, in many instances artificial or contested, unclear or illogical, but – their saving virtue in this time of troubles – facts.

The Congo crisis provided Africa with its first taste of the possibility of a new round of foreign intervention in African affairs, a contest for spheres of influence or domination similar to the partition of the late nineteenth century. This was at the very outset of the liberation process which aimed to get foreigners off its back. To be rid of the Belgians only to open the way for Russians or Americans was no part of any African design, and yet the events of the second half of 1960 created a threat of an independent Russian incursion (outside the scope of UN operations) in support of Lumumba's political heirs in Orientale province. There was therefore a strong incentive for Africans to forswear types of association which mirrored the ideological split between the superpowers. If the superpowers were motivated by ideologies, all the more reason for Africans to steer clear of them and avoid creating states or unions of states predestined by ideology to become tools of outside powers.

The Ghana–Guinea–Mali group, largely fortuitous in its origins, had developed early in the Congo crisis into the Casablanca group which was a merger of West African radicals with North African supporters of the Algerian revolt against France. Opposed to it was the larger Brazzaville group, initially of francophone states and intent primarily on continuing and expanding, in association with France, the common services of the colonial past. The Brazzaville group became in 1961 the Monrovia group by the addition of a number of ex-British territories and the defection of Libya (pre-Gaddafi) from the Casablanca group. The accession of Nigeria in particular sharpened the anti-Casablanca tone of the larger group owing to Nigerian distrust of Nkrumah, while its size – it included twenty states – made it an OAU in embryo.

In May 1963 thirty-one African states, assembled in Addis Ababa, signed the charter of the OAU (see Appendix D). The Organization's first declared aim was to promote the unity of the continent but the charter, by declaring the sovereign equality of all members, also blocked the kind of unity at which Nkrumah's pan-Africanism had been directed. It sanctified the sovereign state and so determined the principles which were to govern the coming proliferation of new states: colonial territories advanced to statehood retaining their colonial boundaries. Twenty years later the OAU had fifty members of this kind, including sovereign islands off the west coast of Africa and in the Indian Ocean but still excluding South Africa's racialist stronghold. Only two major challenges have been made to these principles: over the disposition of Spanish Morocco, disputed at first between Morocco and Mauritania and then by the attempt to create a separate West Saharan state; and in the Horn of Africa where Eritreans have fought for independence from Ethiopia and Somalia for possession of part of it.

But if the charter of the OAU buried political unification it also symbolized surviving unity of purpose. Equipped like the UN and OAS with a standard set of political, economic and cultural organs it has also a body of a special kind: a Liberation Committee established to prosecute the unfinished business of emancipation down to and including the Cape of Good Hope. The colour question and the continuing fight against racialism have given Africans a common concern which no government may wholly ignore and to which some of them give genuine, persistent and practical attention – as witness the role of the so-called Front Line states in bringing independence to Zimbabwe and trying to do the same for Namibia.

The political map of Africa reflects therefore two imported strains – the sovereign state and the international association of sovereign states. The former is a product of European experience and jurisprudence. The latter, of more recent design, has a continental analogue in the Organization of American States but no corresponding body in any other continent: it is rather a United Nations writ small, a geographical association in an area which is nevertheless too big to sustain the functions of an active region. Both forms – the state and the OAU – obscure and downgrade the possible advantages of a third political form, the intermediate regional federation or association which, like the EEC in Europe and ASEAN in Asia, is primarily economic and non-ideological but has also secondary political implications. Regional cooperation of this kind has been stunted in the first post-liberation generation. It may be due for a revival but the sovereign state has become the basic building block and its problems are therefore fundamental to African stability and progress.

3 THE PROBLEM OF GOVERNMENT

I

The states of Africa, committed by the events of a single generation to the responsibilities of national government and the interplay of international relations, suffer grave handicaps which are geographical, economic and institutional. Many of them are ill defined and incoherent. Their poverty is becoming proverbial – a subject to which we will return in the next chapter. They lack a national ruling class, public services and a relevant theory of legitimacy in government; and these political and institutional weaknesses reflect corresponding spiritual and psychological ones, the absence – except in some restricted professional groups, commercial or military – of a national consciousness or national pride. Time may cure all these ills but the future looks a long way off. The present reality is an incapacity which makes nonsense of the neat and tidy picture presented by the map. The states of Africa fall short of what is understood by statehood elsewhere.

By confirming colonial frontiers the new states adopted undemarcated or disputed borders and incorporated religious and ethnic conflicts. In Africa the state's borders, instead of providing its basic definition, emphasize its artificiality. Thus, on borders, Mali with Upper Volta and Mauritania; Benin (ex-Dahomey) with Niger and Nigeria; Gabon with Congo-Brazzaville; Algeria with Morocco; Uganda with Sudan, Kenya and Tanzania; Kenya additionally with Somalia, and Tanzania additionally with Malawi. The great religious divide between Islam and Christianity runs through the huge states of Ethiopia, Sudan, Chad and Nigeria. Bisected tribal groups are too numerous to catalogue; the Ewe who straddle Ghana and Togo and the Azande who straddle Sudan and the Central African Republic are prominent examples of countless overspills. Large minorities (potential Ulsters) perplex government in Zimbabwe, Kenya and other countries. Finally, some countries are just too big for good government, notably where they are not only big but also ethnically diverse and ill provided with communications: as witness, the civil wars in Zaire and Nigeria in the 1960s.

Not all these conflicts are active but none can be put out of mind. If it is surprising that they have given rise to comparatively little fighting, the surprise is a measure of persistent unease and instability.

This is another way of saying that the tasks of government in independent Africa are peculiarly difficult because, among other perplexities, the coherence of its states is more than normally at risk. The rulers face in new states complications which older and more settled societies have escaped or overcome, so that the qualities and credentials of the ruling class are therefore of paramount importance. When Africa was turned into an array of independent states these states needed – besides certain frontiers, internal stability and economic viability – a ruling class.

The dissolution of an empire has most often in modern history cleared the way for the assumption of authority by a ruling class in waiting. Such was the case with the collapse of the first British empire in North America and the Habsburg and Ottoman empires in Europe. The smoothest transfer in terms of bureaucratic competence was effected in the Habsburg lands where imperial rule bequeathed an excellent civil service to the successor states. In North America the extrusion of the British crown and governors left power in the hands of an oligarchy similar to that which ruled England at the time and who knew the ropes. Even in the comparatively backward lands of the Ottoman empire in Europe much of government had long been in European hands and a self-confident middle class was prepared to take over.

But in Africa transition was abrupt and preparation minimal. In Zaire, an extreme but not untypical example, the Belgians withdrew on six months' notice, leaving behind them neither the civil nor the military institutions which a state requires. This was an act of enormous irresponsibility. A few Zairois occupied modest clerical posts in the civil service or held non-commissioned rank in the army. Educational, medical, veterinary and communications services were no better provided. Throughout Africa new states came into existence with an unparalleled lack of state apparatus.

The consequences of this bareness were compounded by suddenness. Both colonizers and colonized had seen the end of colonialism as an instantaneous transfer of power and authority. The date might be uncertain; and so too the degree of violence and bloodshed, but one thing seemed certain to practically everybody. The end, when it came, would come snap. In the morning of a given day there would be a colony; by evening not.

This view of the matter was contested by few. Yet there was an alternative and at least one African statesman saw it. If he had been offered a declaration of independence by a fixed date (say, twenty-five years ahead), coupled with a partnership in the interval, Julius Nyerere of Tanganyika would have accepted it. It is impossible to say whether such an arrangement would have worked. For any African leader to share power with the imperial government and at the same time satisfy his followers would have been a severe test; for the imperial power a condominium would have seemed an unnatural halfway house with authority ambiguously diffused and expenditure imperfectly controlled. More pertinently, the intellectual climate had no room for such ideas. At first sight it may seem strange that British, French and other European colonial servants, who by and large were neither stupid nor cynical, should not have devised better schemes for helping nascent states with the essential business of government – the business in which they themselves took pride. But the decisions to decolonize were taken not by colonial servants but by politicians, most of whom never visited a colony. There was, further, an assumption that offers of help would be resented; and in the aftermath of a great war in which the principal European nations had suffered very severe material loss there was a mood of retrenchment, a feeling (distinctly so in Britain, perhaps less sharp in France) that it was time for somebody else to look after the world, a feeling of relief at the end of empire. Such a mood welcomed neither experiment nor half measures.

Yet, in the British colonies in particular, independence was achieved with a surprising degree of mutual goodwill and the question remains whether this goodwill might not have been put to better use than the superficial compliments and jollity exchanged when black and white saluted each other's flags and danced together at independence balls. In retrospect it looks like an opportunity missed.

This is not to support those who have argued, at the time and since, that independence came too soon and should have been resisted. Merely to postpone independence would have done no more than postpone the problems: by themselves dates are of small account. Opponents of decolonization were seeking excuses for doing nothing largely because they regarded abdication as an admission of weakness, even of guilt, which a major power like Britain or France ought not to entertain. The proponents of inaction argued that the conditions for change – meaning, in effect, the competence of the successors – were not propitious but they advanced no practical proposals for altering those conditions, and this barren opposition could only have exacerbated anti-colonial emotions and the bitterness of an inevitable parting without helping to equip the dependent territories for statehood. The prolongation of negligence is not a remedy for anything.

What the new men took over was not a state but a shell. Independence ceremonies were described over and over again in terms of power being handed over on a plate. In substance, however, there was either little power or no plate. The transition from colonialism to independence could not turn individuals, however intelligent and well intentioned, into statesmen (in the basic meaning of that term) by endowing them with constitutions, flags and national anthems but without the authority and institutions taken for granted in other parts of the world. Never in history have new states been conjured into existence so denuded of the capacity to govern their affairs.

However easily explained by the historian, this negligence cannot be contemplated without sadness. The modern state is a European construct and yet Europeans gave little thought to the conditions for its transplant into Africa. The essence of the modern state is the public service as developed in Europe (and China) by the creation of a civil (i.e. non-military) service to run the state whether it be monarchy, democracy or of any other form. Only on this foundation of competence, pervasiveness and integrity can a state develop the twin prerequisites of progress – order and education – without which nothing gets invented and no economic revolution, industrial or agricultural, is remotely possible. Nor can life itself, liberty or the pursuit of happiness be assured. A society without professional public services is a society in the doldrums whose only alternative to stagnation is a desperate social upheaval which is too often fruitless as well as nasty.

II

The end of the British empire in India not only accelerated the liberation of Africa; it also determined the method. Make up your mind to take the plunge: find your Nehrus and Jinnahs: fix a date and draft a constitution and get out. Local rule will not be as good as British rule but waiting will not make it so and with luck it will be good enough. This attitude may have been more superficially generous than profound, more emotional than intellectual, more expedient than percipient, but it governed British thinking and made its mark on what other Europeans were to do sooner or later in Asia and in Africa. It owed a good deal to Britain's conscious or unconscious awareness that although power in India had not been shared, administration had been (at independence a high proportion of all those in the administrative grades of the government of India were Indians); that Indians had made their appearance in the highest central and provincial councils; and that in commerce, industry and the professions thousands of Indians had substantial experience and status. In India the British handed over power. They did not merely drop it. Their departure had a number of painful and even culpable features but it was not fundamentally irresponsible like the manner of the departure of the Belgians or, in lesser degree, other Europeans from Africa.

So Africa's new states became independent abruptly and at different moments. These two chronological items had important consequences. No less important were two others: most of the new states began life without an acknowledged ruling class and without an accepted theory of government.

The balance sheet of colonialism can never be drawn to universal satisfaction. The attempt is a fruitless exercise, not merely because of the emotions involved but also because it purports to set moral pros and cons alongside material ones – an exercise in illogical incommensurability. Imperial rule brought benefits almost everywhere; they included security of movement, destruction of pests (locust control, for example), new techniques, better communications, some education, the enforcement of criminal law. But in government there is a heavy legacy of debit.

The very existence of imperial power downgrades traditional rulers, good as well as bad. The imposition of a colonial regime inevitably discredited whatever preceded it and inhibited the development of nascent states and nascent national feeling. It encouraged a divisive tribalization, sometimes as a useful political device and sometimes out of romantic preconception, but tending in either case to the fragmentation of the colonial territory and the negation of any kind of nationwide legitimacy. Kingship, as in Buganda or the Muslim emirates of West Africa or Swaziland, was treated with respect but politically emasculated; the only monarchy to survive more or less intact was the Moroccan. To the age-old question *Quo Warranto?* – By what right do you rule? – the new men who took the place of the colonial power had no convincing answer.

Government in Africa has therefore been above all else weak. This does not mean that it has not been in places authoritarian, as distinct from authoritative, or even violent: examples come all too readily to mind, civilian (Banda, Kenyatta) as well as military (Bokassa, Mobutu, Amin). But strong men do not necessarily make strong government. The problem of corruption makes the point. All governments decry corruption – even when they exempt themselves and their relatives. One way to end corruption is by stamping on it. The Ottoman sultan Selim I did so, for example, in a short reign of eight years. But no African government has been able to do so and those which have given themselves high-sounding titles like National Redemption Council to back their military power have been as ineffective as any. After a few years they have faded away with nothing accomplished. While they may be excused for doing no better with the economy than the civilians whom they oust, their inability to stem corruption speaks volumes for their inherent incapacity as rulers.

A second example, of which more will be said later, is the inability of governments to master the rural peasantry on whom their economies depend. They have failed to persuade and they have failed to coerce, and almost universally they have seen agricultural production fail to keep pace with the needs of the population and the agricultural population leave the land. The causes of these and similar failures are diverse but central to them is the lack of authority. Even when the rulers knew what they wanted they could not achieve it. (An apparent exception, in Ghana after the return of a million Ghanaians evicted from Nigeria in 1982, is a dubious one. These workless re-entrants returned to their villages but were forced to do so by the desperate hopelessness of the coastal economy as much as by the will or authority of government. They left again as soon as they could.)

It cannot be too frequently emphasized that the rulers' tasks were unprecedented. To acquire lasting authority on the instant is formidably difficult, and in Africa it has been rendered the more difficult by the rejection of two tested sources of legitimacy: *vox Dei* and *vox populi*.

The European state, which is the ancestor of the *genus*, acquired definition and stability by adopting the artificial principle of an hereditary and semi-divine monarchy, combined with the secondary principle of primogeniture. This system has its defects – the odd imbecile, lecher, crook – but they were outweighed by the virtue of certainty until, with time, Europe could base something more logical on this stability. Primogeniture was adopted in the Middle Ages as an extra element in certainty. The Merovings, for example, did not have it; their successors in France added it to make assurance doubly sure. In more sheltered England, where the idea of the semi-divine royal family held sway from soon after the departure of the Romans, primogeniture did not become the rule until the late twelfth century when it was imported by the tidy-minded Plantagenets. Primogeniture reduced the need for the sanction of divinity and so accelerated the secularization of monarchy in Europe. Tsarist Russia did not have it.

Primogeniture is one way of buttressing an hereditary system but not the only way. It secures certainty at some cost in efficiency. The strictly monarchical and primogenital system excludes any element of choice (unless the Macedonian institution of brother–sister marriage is counted as an instance of human intervention in an essentially superhuman dispensation). Whereas Europe put its money on fixed rules of succession, Islam preferred to buttress its hereditary system by efficiency at some cost in certainty. The caliph had to come from the Prophet's family but, notably in the theory and practice of the Zaidi branch of the Alid stem, performance mattered as well as birth; this was a way of diluting heredity with a dash of capability, still within a narrow group, in an attempt to get the better man, even at some cost in stability. (The Kharijites went so far as to reject the claims of a privileged family altogether.)

This derogation from the strictest hereditary principle raised the question: performance at what? If the ruler's title is to be legitimized by his actions, what is it that he is required to be good at? Until virtually the present day the answer was easy: the ruler's main function has been to keep order and be good at war. Failure to keep order is a self-evident disqualification of a ruler besides visiting countless discomforts on the ruled. Failure in war, or even the failure to display martial qualities in peace time, has repeatedly led to the removal of the ruler to the cloister or to his grave because he has proved himself unfit for his main job.

It would be foolishly premature to claim that flag-waving, scabbard-rattling and gun-boating are no longer a title to prestige and power. Even the most mature and pacific countries prove sporadically receptive to primitive passions. But by and large rulers in the modern world are judged, and are honoured or destroyed, by a different touchstone: the way they care for their people's health and wealth rather than by their prowess in inflicting death and destruction on their neighbours. In other words, their title is tested by their economic performance. Providing stability and victory is no longer enough. In the past military failure has been followed by disorders and even revolution. Now, economic failure may do the same.

This is another piece of bad luck for African rulers since, as will appear in the next chapter, they have inherited terrible economic problems.

The new men have been far from negligible personalities. They have won for themselves the title to leadership called charisma and they have won it by action. But the action became, upon independence, historical. It continued for a while to shed glamour but it ceased to be relevant to post-colonial problems; and the title so conferred could be neither shared nor passed on. The charismatic leader counted for more than his movement or organization, for the qualities which gave him his charisma were above all personal. The colonial situation called for a flamboyance which could enthuse Africans and scare Europeans, for the politics of liberation were a crusade which turned into a negotiation only because the Europeans recognized the force of the crusade and took the decision to give way to it, to show the crusaders politely into the seats of power.

On the African side leadership, whether rhetorical or intellectual or a combination of both, was more telling than the virtues of a committee chairman or an administrator. But, however xenophobic, it was rarely revolutionary. These men came mostly from a small professional class, with fairly restricted regional roots: narrowly based therefore socially and geographically but radical only in a whiggish or (in the British sense) liberal mode. Outside the Islamic north revolutionary currents were all but invisible. Sub-Saharan leaders were reformers who were opposed to traditional chiefs and customs as impediments to progress and unworthy, anachronistic representatives of the new Africa. But they lacked the innate authority of these very chiefs and those of them who came from chiefly stock owed their positions to other sources – superior education or, particularly in the French colonies, association with a foreign commercial or administrative elite. Their instrument was a movement which was popular in theory but restricted in numbers and urban rather than rural: the leaders were townees.

This instrument, like the colonial rule against which it was pitted, was monolithic. It was also new. No African political movement had anything approaching the lifespan of the Indian Congress Party or the elaborate organization which made the Congress a training ground for independent India's public services. African leaders and their parties served their apprenticeship in a situation in which other groups competing with them were regarded as traitors to the cause of independence and, after independence, as traitors to national solidarity. At liberation the victorious movement accepted a constitution under which it was to be transformed into a party in a system which presupposed the existence of other parties: the British were particularly solicitous in equipping their ex-colonies with multi-party systems on the assumption that such a system is inherently good (true) and appropriate (not necessarily true). A dominant feature of Africa since independence has been the destruction of these systems. So the rulers' inherent lack of legitimacy has been compounded by their ostensible, initial attachment to a system which they have then abandoned, not without the appearance of inconsistency and compulsion. A number of them merely increased their power but not their authority.

A multi-party system is superior to the one-party state because it is a defence against tyranny or, leaving aside the harsher aspects of tyranny, against selfish or myopic rule. It is a device for securing justice as well as order, and its abandonment signals a need to assert order, if necessary at the expense of justice. A benevolent ruler, whether an enlightened despot of the eighteenth century or a Nyerere or Kaunda of the twentieth, will try to preserve justice in other ways; but these are intrinsically frailer. In Tanzania Nyerere's liberation movement TANU (in association with the Afro-Shirazi party of Zanzibar) was gradually substituted for the state; its executive committee superseded in effect the parliament and Tanzania became constitutionally a one-party state. But TANU's regional committees frequently belied Nyerere's benevolence and dealt harshly with people who were deprived of effective redress. Zambia also became in 1973 officially a one-party state at the instance of a leader no less democratically inclined than Nyerere but afraid of losing his grip. Kenneth Kaunda hoped to preserve political life in local organs of planning and government but few were drawn in and the outcome was the creation of local elites or cliques with enough power to exercise petty tyranny but not enough to get anything done. In both these states government became weaker and almost certainly nastier. Yet they were among the most respectable in Africa. Their shortcomings reflected not vice but incapacity.

The case for the one-party state in Africa or anywhere else is that party political strife weakens government by producing too much verbosity and too little action. The elimination of faction – which is branded as a luxury – therefore clears the way for the government to get on with its business. In addition, party in Africa has often been equated with separatism and secession. The net result is to sanction civilian autocracy in the name of national solidarity, efficiency and progress. The counter-argument is that a self-perpetuating oligarchy of this kind may be efficient but gives free rein to arrogance and greed and confines progress, if any, to the favoured few. In practice the question is how much arrogance and greed will be excused and tolerated in return for how much efficiency. And as soon as this question is posed there are the makings of a new and potentially more violent factionalism.

Military rule is a variant on the same theme. Where some states have converted to a one-party system others have succumbed to a military rule, which is a special kind of one-party system (so long as the armed forces hold together). It is usually overt with military men seated in the visible places of power, but sometimes indirect with civilians retained as a front for the exercise of the military will. The main engine of the shift to military rule has been the failure of the antecedent civilian government to perform, thus releasing regional or tribal discontents. The sequence began in Togo in 1963 with the assassination of President Sylvanus Olympio whose successor, Nicholas Grunitzky, lasted four years before being displaced in his turn by the real strong man Etienne Eyadema. Togo subsequently enjoyed comparative stability, political and economic, but elsewhere in West and Central Africa military coups have become an established way to change the government, partly to satisfy the ambitions or indignations of generals, colonels or even sergeants, and partly because the constitutional machinery for change did not work or was not allowed to work: the military were the obvious, frequently the only, alternative to a civilian government which refused to be removed in any other way or had no obvious replacement in waiting. The military had too the reputation of being comparatively free of corruption and ideological claptrap and more clearly embodied a national rather than a regional or tribal spirit. (This was not always the case. The Ugandan army had a strong regional bias and Colonel Lamizana's coup in Upper Volta in 1966 a strong ideological flavour. In Benin – then still Dahomey – the device adopted in 1970 of a rotating group of three military chiefs from different regions recognized without abating tribal rifts and was in any case short lived.)

Military rule in Africa has been noted either for its excesses (Idi Amin, Jean-Bedel Bokassa, Francisco Macias Nguema) or for its inadequacies (Ghana had four military regimes in sixteen years but none of them stemmed corruption or economic decline). This record may help to explain why, in spite of its prevalence, it has continued to be regarded as an unwelcome interruption to the norm of civilian rule. The strongest military rulers, in Nigeria for example, have been the most insistent on their wish to return to barracks and did actually do so. Another motive has been the discovery that they are no more able than the civilians to produce what is expected of governments. Nigeria did not become more orderly or safer for the ordinary citizen under military rule, nor did it become an exemplar of efficiency and integrity. In Ghana Flight Lieutenant Rawlings, who twice seized power as a modern Saviour with the Sword, raised expectations which he has failed to satisfy, thus adding to the general discredit of government. Under his rule indisciplined army units spread terror in the countryside and villagers fled either into the bush or across the borders into neighbouring states to the east, west and north. In spite of some rise in the world price of cocoa the Ghanaian crop remained unmarketed because the price received did not cover the farmer's costs or because, even if the farmer did take what he could get, there was nothing for him to buy with the money and he was liable to have his home invaded by soldiers who accused him of hoarding, beat him and robbed him. Africa has learnt the hard way that military rule is no more successful than civilian rule and a good deal more disagreeable.

Military rule stifles conflicts which a democratic civilian regime seeks to manage. In either case the conflicts persist. New states have a special problem. If, as is the case in Africa, they do not embody a nation, they need to form one. The elites, particularly governing and intellectual elites, are wedded to the idea of the nation state, but it is not at all clear that the idea is more widespread than that. In the absence of a common language – the focus of European statehood – loyalties are basically to tribes. They are not sloughed off when people move away from tribal homelands and into cities, since the urban migrants gravitate to their tribal kin and reproduce in the city the tribal groupings to which they traditionally respond. This natural instinct of kinship is reinforced when the urban politician in search of votes appeals to it even though, ostensibly intent on building a nation, he privately scouts such antiquated loyalties. The party politician appealing to what he does not believe in adds to the incoherence of the African state.

III

To look at Africa in terms of European conquerors retreating from colonial territories which they turn into modern pseudo-states is to forget Islam.

The northern slice of Africa was Islamicized long before the arrival of the first modern European traders, adventurers or rulers, and in this context northern Africa includes much of West and East Africa. The Muslim influence is profound – a circumstance that has been obscured by the relatively short-lived events of the nineteenth century. In the fifty years after 1830 the French spread over most of Muslim Africa west of the Nile; the imposition of a French protectorate over Morocco in 1912 was the tailpiece to this pervasive but, as it turned out, ephemeral expansion. In the same period the British secured control over the Anglo-Egyptian Sudan and then over the Muslim emirates which had been part of the West African empire of Uthman dan Fodio and his followers.

But these Europeans, however much they blanketed Islam, did not suppress it or try to, and since their departure the significance of Islam to Africa has grown because it appears to have entered on a new hyperactive phase in its history and because it has a theory of the state which is at odds with the political theories dangled before Africans by the European interlopers of the nineteenth century.

The Muslim state is in theory an instrument of the divine purpose. It is subordinate to and guided by the divine law (sharia), tempered by the historical experience (sunna) of Muhammad and his immediate followers and by reason. It supervises and restrains human imperfection and is therefore a restrictive rather than a liberal instrument. It acknowledges a principle of justice (and so distinguishes between good rulers and bad) but not the validity of *vox populi*. Unlike European Christianity, Islam has not had to agonize over the distinction between church and state; if and so far it has done so, it subjects the latter to the former (most insistently in *shia* doctrine and practice as exemplified today by Ayatollah Khomeini in Iran).

Muslim theory has had a rough passage through history. In practice Islamic states have quickly become repositories of secular power in which the king has been mightier than the priest and *raison d'état* has overridden or at least attenuated the precepts of the faith. In this respect the long centuries of Ottoman Turkish pre-eminence only reinforced a trend that was already evident as early as the Abbasid caliphate in Baghdad.

But not decisively. Muslims – that is to say, persons distinguished by their religion rather than their secular citizenship – remain a class apart from non-Muslims. The numerous constitutions of Pakistan since independence have all proclaimed it an Islamic state in much the same spirit as the Muslim emperor Aurungzeb's reforms put Hindus in their place in the seventeenth century. Modern Turkey, a generation after the death of its creator Kemal Ataturk, has fallen into endemic turmoil because of the resurgence of those pretensions of religion which Kemal wanted to divorce from the state. The very idea of the finite state accords uneasily with Islamic tradition, as witness not only Gaddafi's cavalier attitude to state frontiers but also the Muslim Brotherhood and the Baath – competing movements which nevertheless concur in their disregard of state boundaries and so recall the non-territorial crusading enthusiasms which animated Uthman dan Fodio or the Sudan's Mahdi in an earlier age. Politically Islam is a destabilizing force because, quite apart from any resurgence of radical fundamentalism, it has failed to resolve the tensions between secular and clerical authority, has given the victory to neither and is ambivalent about the legitimacy of the secular state.

Of these disruptive factors Gaddafi is an extreme illustration, bewildering as well as irritating and scaring his enemies. Gaddafi, a fervent Muslim, goes so far as to make a virtue of the non-state. Eight years after the revolution which brought him to power in 1969 he abolished the state, its conventional institutions and the notion of fixed frontiers. The renaming of embassies abroad as People's Bureaux – a move greeted in foreign capitals with disdain and derision – was merely one aspect of a deliberate extension of an anarchical populism which has made Libya one of the few African countries to experience a revolution as well as a transfer of power. The makers of the 1969 coup, comparatively lowly officers from minor tribes, were animated by a message and determined to inaugurate a genuinely broad popular sovereignty. Superficially, xenophobia gave their movement some resemblance to the anti-colonialism of the rest of Africa and they began by making the changes which are the standard hallmarks of independence from foreign rule: removal of foreign bases, nationalization of financial and commercial enterprises. But their main purpose was larger. They prohibited all political parties on the grounds that they are the emanations of class interests and put in their place regional, supposedly classless, bodies in an attempt to create a communal as opposed to a party-political democracy. Gaddafi's political ideas owe something to Pakistan's constitutional experiments and something to Nasser's but little, if anything, to Leninist leadership-from-the-top communism.

Like all true revolutionaries Gaddafi wants to export his ideas and this impetus (reminiscent of the first years of the French Revolution) partly explains the political unions which he fruitlessly projected with other countries year after year. The cash from Libya's providential discoveries of oil in the 1970s, and the paucity of Libya's population and domestic needs, helped to keep Gaddafi's experiments from foundering, but his devolved democracy has been a mirage and power has rested not with the people but with the army: the people seem to care little about power, the army much. So Libya has become a state masquerading as a non-state and parading extravagant notions, but how prophetically or ephemerally remains to be seen. It exhibits aspects of Islamic tradition but may well follow Islamic experience in reverting to a more conventional central government, military or civilian, within a territorially defined state which recognizes other secular states and eschews imperial and religious visions (which, with its small population, it cannot possibly bring into being).

But if Gaddafi, as a statesman, is unpractical and anachronistic, Islam has a supranational impact which is stronger than anything which Europe or Christendom has produced for centuries. Pan-Islam is more than a word. (Strictly speaking it is a tautology since Islam *ipso verbo* is singular and all-embracing.) Its symbol was the caliphate and during the nineteenth century there was much debate in the Muslim world about the future of the caliphate. After the First World War the caliphate was extinguished as a result of Turkey's defeat and Kemal's secularism, but some of the notions which it embodied have been revived by the Saudi royal house. King Feisal (reigned 1964–75), already custodian of the holiest Muslim places, institutionalized a Standing Islamic Conference as a sign of Muslim unity – or at least the desirability and potential force of such unity. Significantly it is a conference of states and to that extent a concession to the ways of the modern, state-ridden world, an attempt – like the OAU – to impose a limited unity on a fragmented world but with religion and not geography as its determining feature, potentially a catalyst in contradistinction to the inertia of a geographical association.

The core of modern Islamic unity is Arab and Middle Eastern. The Arab states, dynastic and others, have common political concerns in their hostility to Israel and their nervousness about the designs of the superpowers on their strategically crucial homelands. The unity of the wider Muslim world is much less easy to envisage or achieve and must be religious rather than political: it is, for example, hard to discern any common political purposes shared by Indonesia and Morocco. But it would be imprudent to overlook the power of Islam to create and sustain a combined international impetus at a time when that religion is making so much more noise in the world than any other.

A large part of Africa belongs to this world. Tens of thousands of Nigerians, to give a single example, make the pilgrimage to Mecca every year. Conflicts in East Africa have religious roots: Saudi and

Sudanese Muslims have given aid to Eritreans against Ethiopia's Christian ruling caste, Somali/Ethiopian fighting is invested with religious slogans and Somali/Kenyan conflict could be so too. Megalomaniacs as diverse as Gaddafi and King Hassan of Morocco dream of vast empires conquered for the faith – or at least by the faithful – and the fancifulness of these visions does not make them the less disturbing to the peace of the area. Egypt, the most important Muslim country, is suspended between a broadly tolerant form of the faith and the radical fundamentalism which has captured Iran and knows no frontiers. The whole of northern Africa must be influenced by the way Egypt goes.

What Islam offers in the closing decades of the twentieth century is, on the one hand, a society and state which are authoritarian but broadly tolerant, religious but not priest-ridden, and monarchic–oligarchic; on the other hand a revolutionary current which, also religious and authoritarian, is ruthless, narrow, expansionist and hostile to foreign (specially western) cultures and technologies. The assertion of Muslim power in either form over northern Africa would threaten the continental unity which Africans have nurtured in order to keep the peace in their continent and to increase their bargaining weight in the rest of the world.

It threatens too the stability of those states where Muslim and non-Muslim societies co-exist in roughly equal strength. Chief of these is Nigeria where the problem was already present to the minds of the British at the beginning of this century. British colonial rulers had considerable respect for princely institutions and used them within the context of indirect rule. The Yoruba obas of Western Nigeria came into this category but the British wished also to steer Nigeria towards a representative parliamentary democracy into which the obas did not easily fit. The obas were undoubtedly persons of consequence but, like many of the Indian rajahs, not necessarily abreast of the times or particularly alive to popular needs or sympathetic to popular rights. Since they owed their positions to birth and not to popular choice their status in a modern state was questionable. Like bishops in modern Italy they were an influence which could not be ignored but which was in important ways out of date. To make matters more difficult for the British the obas kept each to his own (sometimes very small) patch and so did not constitute a composite political force. The British were reluctant openly to urge them into politics over a wider field for fear of appearing to make use of them and so, by turning them into stooges, reducing an influence which they wished to sustain. The danger, which has persisted after the

British retreat, was of setting a traditional elite against an emergent modern elite.

The British sponsored the creation of a conference of Western Nigerian Chiefs which evolved into a piece of constitutional machinery. This development recognized the intrinsic importance of the chiefs but pointed also towards a dyarchy – chiefs on the one hand, a parliament on the other – which was bound to be awkward as well as unfashionable. The Nigerian constitution of 1979 created a unicameral system at the centre and in the several states but also perpetuated the special position of chiefs through provincial Councils of Chiefs with restricted advisory functions. In Western and Northern Nigeria these Councils embody some of the supervisory and regulatory functions of the Muslim tradition. On paper they are clearly subordinate to the organs of the secular state but not all Muslims see it that way and so long as Islam's bonds remain strong there is in such societies a body of potential support for a very different kind of state, whether monarchical like Saudi Arabia or theocratic like Iran. Both have roots in Africa.

Africa's Islamic flavour has therefore political as well as religious impact. The religious divide between Muslims and Christians is an open and accepted fact. Less well recognized is the variety of the political patterns which Muslims and Christians have brought to a continent whose indigenous political forms have been stunted by alien rule and depreciated by modern example.

4 THE ECONOMIC TRAP

I

If the main business of governments in post-liberation Africa is the fulfilment of economic expectations, and if at the same time these governments are weak to the point of incoherence, then their economic performance is certain to be poor. But an economic review of modern Africa cannot start with the state of governments, since governments themselves start with what they inherit.

This inheritance is two-fold: natural and colonial. Africa is not poor. Parts of it are appallingly poor but other parts are fertile and mineral wealth – most of it in the south and northwest – is lavish. This is a continent of extremes.

The colonial contribution was mixed and in some respects poisoned. No colonial regime has ever undertaken the administration of a distant territory with the aim of improving the lot of its inhabitants. On the other hand it is wrong to maintain that that lot has never been improved. The most illuminating example of what a colonial power may do is India under British rule. The introduction and enforcement of criminal law was a great blessing from the insistence that, for example, thuggee is murder to the widespread imposition of the rule of law in everyday affairs over large areas. The introduction and enforcement of the law of contract was a more debatable boon in so far as it sanctioned the proposition that one can and should get blood from a stone: it not only helped creditors to get even with reluctant or crooked debtors but also placed creditors in a position to imprison genuinely helpless debtors or seize their goods and land – a form of justice which, although it may satisfy the legal mind, leaves the social conscience uneasy.

The British in India laid down a network of communications – railways and harbour works – which benefited the country as well as themselves: the civil aspect of the law and order imposed in the first place by superior power. These works were built with British money. (British capital also laid the foundations of American industry in the nineteenth century. These are examples, not of the play of morality in public affairs, but of what one country's money has in fact done for another.) Good communications are essential both to the functioning of a country-wide economy and to its government: communications of one kind or another are a pre-condition for government whether the central power proposes to exert authority by sending letters or by sending soldiery. The fact that India today has a better postal service than the United States is thanks to the British and no small boon.

In Africa the British and other Europeans were concerned with law and order both because disorder impeded their own (mainly commercial) purposes and because they were revolted by the grosser forms of lawlessness and disorder. There was a powerful humanitarian ingredient alongside the search for gain; greed and compassion are not wholly incompatible, neither among stern Victorians nor yet today. But the economic impact on Africa was very different from the Indian case. India is a case apart as well as an illustration.

The members of Britain's Indian Civil Service spent their entire working lives in India. But no colonial servant spent his life in a particular colony or even in the same continent or knew any territory half as well as the Indian civil servant knew his. The focus of a career in the colonies was the service, not the place. Secondly, the government of India under the Governor-General (later the Viceroy) was a powerful and efficient central administration with ideas of its own, sometimes at variance with the policies of the India Office in London, and the British Cabinet to a degree unthinkable in the relations between a colonial governor and the Colonial Office. The government of India, which was in India, saw India whole and was capable of putting India's interests above those of British traders and capitalists, whom it not infrequently despised. Thus Indian railways were laid out to subserve the Indian economy, whereas in Africa communications were planned either to get the produce of a small favoured area to the coast and so away to Europe (a series of drains rather than a network) or for strategic purposes (the Mombasa–Lake Victoria line, for example).

The essence of the charge against colonial economics is that the colonizer was attracted to the colony by its resources and his business was the removal of these resources. Specially chosen areas were developed and stripped – annually if they were agricultural, until exhausted if they were mineral. Markets in neighbouring African territories were not developed and the colony became increasingly riveted to the economy of the metropole, as a flourishing but dependent modern economy was inserted into the colony alongside the stagnant traditional economy. The profits of the former were garnered by the foreigner and by a small elite of African farmers, traders and chiefs while the wider economy benefited not at all because taxation of profits was light or evadable or non-existent. But – a significant fact overlooked by the post-liberation rulers – some capital and technology were introduced. However narrow the motives of the providers, the consequences of their provision were wider.

To the ruled the shortcomings of the rulers are more obvious than their beneficence, and this psychological propensity is all the stronger when the rulers are foreign. When new rulers took over in Africa they had to make choices, to adopt economic policies which essentially either continued the policies of the colonial era or broke with them; and in making these choices no ruler could be wholly uninfluenced by the fact that colonialism was popularly regarded as the root of all evil. Yet – and this has been a central dilemma for Africans – any attempt to transform the economy from colonial exploitation to a more autonomous and profitable development required extensive help from the outside world, including the former colonial powers. Development, particularly industrialization but also agricultural development, required not only technical advice and supervision but considerable sums of foreign money. Economically and psychologically development in the first decades of independence was industrialization which, however appealing to the ruling few, was both alien to Africans in general and specially dependent on foreign funds and goodwill. (The story of West African bauxite, to be related below, becomes in this context a parable of blighted hopes and justified blind prejudice.)

Within the conditioning restraints of this complex inheritance the new rulers of Africa had to fashion strategies to achieve certain ends. These ends were easy to list but less easy to arrange in an order of priority. They were, in broad outline, to maintain and improve the agricultural base in order to feed a growing population and, where possible, enrich its diet and produce a surplus for export; to exploit mineral wealth on the most favourable terms obtainable in order to boost the national product, export earnings and the state's international muscle; and to create, congruently with these two aims, an industrial manufacturing sector.

Put even more simply, this complex of purposes entailed striking a balance between industry and agriculture and finding the resources, domestic or external, to develop the resulting mix. There was also an impulse, political and humane, to move fast. This impulse pointed to industry rather than the traditionally slow-moving rural sector, to the engine rather than the bullock cart. It was a lure which few were minded to resist.

Industrialization, linked in popular belief with modernization and affluence, carries with it a universal promise of economic power and betterment. As a panacea and a badge of progress it is a bequest from the historical experience of Western Europe and North America. It owes more to the past of these corners of the world than to an economic analysis of the here and now in today's Third World. Yet countries all over the world have set themselves to redress, through industrial modernization, the extremes of imbalance between the few advanced industrial states and the rest of mankind, to beat the leaders at their own game. This impetus has been particularly sharp in newly emancipated countries where economic backwardness has been blamed on the shackles imposed by the self-interest of the colonial power. If colonialism kept the colony back, independence must open the way for a leap forward.

After twenty years the fallacies of this diagnosis have become sickeningly obvious. In the first place the business of transforming an economy was vastly underrated. The ship of state responds to economic steering about as rapidly as a giant tanker responds to a touch on the tiller – which is to say with majestic slowness and after a good stretch of inertial progress on its original (sometimes collision) course. In addition, African economies could be converted only by recognizing and mastering two dominant problems among a host of lesser ones. These were, first, the need for external aid in capital, training and technology and the need therefore to secure this aid on terms acceptable to the provider as well as fair to the recipient; and, second, the need to ensure that the peasantry – the bulk of the population and the arbiters of the economy's essentially agricultural base – should have a profitable place in the new economy and should not come to regard government policies as alien to their interests. But the new rulers were ill disposed to both these crucially important groups: the foreign capitalist and the native peasant. They had reasons for their prejudices but misjudged the consequences of following them. Suspicion of the foreign capitalist, grounded in the colonial experience, was magnified by some unhappy dealings after independence with national and multi-national foreign corporations. As foreigner and capitalist he was a twice-dyed adversary. Yet new states could hardly do without him and were ill trained to outwit him. Instead they made life difficult for him, thus either scaring him away or sharpening his knavery. The small farmers too were alienated or simply not sufficiently helped or regarded, and as elsewhere in the world they proved to be a more potent economic force than their town cousins imagined.

In the first years of independence economic problems were partially obscured because the postwar international economic climate had been comparatively benign. The dimensions of problems to come were not apparent. Replenishing the shortages created by the Second World War kept the demand for African products high and their price healthy. But these trends were already being reversed during the 1960s, the decade of most decolonization. Worldwide inflation curbed African exports and forced African rulers and planners to concentrate on import substitution and turn in on themselves. A revival of demand in the early 1970s was more than annulled by the hefty rises in fuel prices from 1973, exceptionally frightful droughts, renewed and more profound world depression, and unstable prices for raw materials.

In these alarming decades African states went several ways. Some continued the colonial pattern. One, Gabon, became an example of posthumous colonialism: a poor country struggling on the proceeds of forestry discovered that it had oil, uranium and manganese, acquired a vast income for a tiny population, allowed its lumbering and agriculture to languish, but provided the bulk of its people with neither employment nor a better living. Other countries opted for industrialization, usually in a capitalist system. Yet others preferred, or were left, to cultivate meagre rural resources, often in a more or less socialist framework. Three West African neighbours illustrate the variety of responses; two East African neighbours supplement the picture.

II

Guinea, Ivory Coast and Ghana occupy most of the coast and its immediate hinterland between the Gambia and Volta rivers (Sierra Leone and Liberia interrupting but not preventing Guinea's access to the sea). Of these three Ivory Coast became (with Kenya in East Africa) the outstanding example of the successful prolongation of the colonial and capitalist pattern – successful within limits which gradually obtruded themselves. Ivory Coast had a number of initial advantages: a good climate, no deserts, manageable size, modest population (8 million) spread at an average density of 15 to the square kilometre, a rural economy not dependent on a single crop. As the largest African exporter of palm oil and the second largest exporter of cocoa Ivory Coast had no serious balance of payments problem and supplemented these exports with coffee, bananas, pineapples and textiles. The national product increased steadily year by year both before independence and after it and income per head also rose, dramatically although far from evenly. The new state avoided costly ostentatious projects and burdensome military expenditure. It refused, selfishly as other Africans claimed, to enter into associations with less favoured states and was determined above all to assert its independence against Senegal which the French had made the centre of their West African empire. In effect its rulers continued the colonial pattern and the partnership with France because it paid to do so – paid, that is, the favoured few with an expectation or hope that their prosperity would produce dividends for everybody else; and in this spirit Abidjan was happy to play host to more French men and women than had worked there before independence. Statisticians applauded this resolve. But there was another side to the coin which led critics to assert that the colonial pattern could be extended for a limited time only and furthermore that its benefits remained narrowly distributed: growth without development.

In one particular Ivory Coast displayed a neat example of the distortion of a colonial economy in the interests of the metropole. The French boosted the cultivation of coffee in order that French men and women might get their staple drink cheap. The principal source of supply was Brazil and other parts of Latin America where conditions for growing coffee are more suitable than in West Africa. French encouragement of coffee growing in Ivory Coast led to overproduction, competition for markets and so lower prices with the Ivorian farmers engaged therefore in fighting Brazilians instead of using their land for crops more appropriate to their soil and climate and with a possible market in Africa instead of only in France.

Presiding over these developments was the PDCI – Parti Démocrate de la Côte d'Ivoire – which began as a rural amalgam to which were added urban elites and non-Ivorians. The party became the government because it established itself as the organization which could deal with the French as their abdication loomed. Its leader, Félix Houphouet-Boigny, was an establishment figure socially and politically. He was a socialist of elevated tribal ancestry who, immediately after the Second World War, had been prominent in creating the Rassemblement Démocratique Africain (RDA), an association of anti-colonial movements from different French colonies, within which he led a socialist opposition to communist groups. He had been a Minister in Paris during the Fourth Republic. His PDCI governed by combining tight state control over parastatal bodies with pecuniary enticement of foreign capital, and he provided the country with a high degree of stability based on his personal authority and pronounced, if lopsided, growth. The westernized elites and commercial and rural tycoons flourished either in business or politics or both, an oligarchy with a rare degree of authority, dispensing orderliness, building up some domestic capital and hoping that good times would continue.

But Houphouet-Boigny was not immortal and growth came to a halt. From a regular 8 or 9 per cent a year it fell to nil in 1981. It had been underwritten by exports produced with the aid of foreign money and foreign labour, the first mainly French and the other attracted from neighbouring African countries. The labour gave rise to internal dissension and to trouble with the neighbours (particularly Upper Volta which had once been a part of Ivory Coast) and the money began to dry up as returns on investment diminished. Domestic savings were not enough to fill the gap, so that the policy failed to generate new sources to keep it going. The balance of payments worsened because of falls in world prices for cocoa and coffee, an accumulation of foreign debt requiring to be serviced, and increased imports of food, commodities and luxuries: by the beginning of the 1980s the debt service required $5 billion a year and absorbed a third of foreign earnings. The increase in imports was occasioned partly by the demands of the better off who were prospering in the modernized sector of the economy but also by the failure of agriculture to keep pace with the needs of the growing population as farmers drifted away from the land and into towns where they hoped to find work and wages to replace yields from the land which were no longer matching their costs. The population of Abidjan rose from 46,000 in 1945 to 1 million or more by 1980 (foreign workers included). One quarter of the total population was foreign, including 80,000 Lebanese traders, natural targets for native discontent in a recession.

The flagging economy ceased to act as a guarantor of order and stability, the more so since its decline coincided with the approaching end of the rule of the octogenarian Houphouet-Boigny (born in the nineteenth century) and an unsettled succession to be determined by no fixed rules.

Like many other countries Ivory Coast is looking to oil for salvation – in other words, for a radical transformation of its economy the easy way. It hopes to become self-sufficient in oil by 1983–84, an exporter in 1985–86. If this lifeline were to fail, then it seems likely to follow the course of its neighbours, Liberia and Ghana, where the advent of Samuel Doe and Jerry Rawlings, military mavericks of a younger generation, signified the collapse of the old economy without any clear prescription for the future.

Ivory Coast has had a counterpart in East Africa – in Kenya, which likewise acquired, in the first phase of independence, a reputation for good order and economic growth. Its colonial pattern was distinguished from others, both favourably and unfavourably, by the white settler element introduced at the beginning of the century and boosted by government policy after the First World War. The settlers were responsible for the development of a prosperous agriculture in the White Highlands and along the coast. Like Ivory Coast, Kenya was dominated at independence and until his death by a single personality, Jomo Kenyatta. Although very different in temperament and experience both Kenyatta and Houphouet-Boigny possessed authority. Kenyatta's authority derived from his unchallenged leadership of the dominant Kikuyu, reinforced by his personal qualities and by an agriculture and commerce prospering in a pre-independence capitalist framework. The British transferred power, in fact if not in intention, to the Kikuyu who carried on in much the same way as their colonial predecessors, although at first with some of the language and institutions of parliamentary democracy. But Kenyatta used his hold over the state to benefit his tribe and family rather than the nation. Corruption became blatant, stability was short lived and in retrospect the Kenyatta years (1963–78) look like wasted years.

Kenyatta's successor was Daniel Moi of the minor Kalenjin tribe. Moi seemed both well placed and personally inclined to inaugurate a more even handed regime. He was a bridge for a chasm; but the chasm was widening faster than the bridge grew. Originally chairman of Kadu, the amalgamated opposition to the mainly Kikuyu Kanu, Moi was brought by Kenyatta into his government and became vice-president and then president. He represented orderly continuity together with the hope that he might temper the irregularities and corruption of the Kenyatta period without endangering its comparative stability. But the stability was superficial: Moi inherited an opposition which had been suppressed but not conciliated.

The main tribal opposition came from the Luo whose principal leaders, Tom Mboya and Oginga Odinga, had been included in Kenyatta's first government but then downgraded. Mboya, who represented a modernizing urban element, was murdered in 1969 with strong indications of Kikuyu involvement. Odinga, who represented the Luos' provincial grass roots, moved into opposition and was discredited after becoming implicated in a plot to overthrow Kenyatta's regime with the help of Soviet arms. After Kenyatta's death Moi encouraged Odinga to seek re-election to parliament but then recoiled when Odinga, with accustomed impetuosity, launched into fresh bitter attacks on the self-seeking corruption of the Kikuyu elite.

In 1982 all parties other than Kanu were banned and Kenya became formally what it had been to all intents and purposes from its earliest days – a one-party state. In the same year the largely Kikuyu Air Force staged a coup which, although an incompetent failure, gravely weakened Moi. This turmoil had more sources than one. Kenyatta's failure to make the best use of his personal authority went hand in hand with a decline in Kenya's economic condition. After independence parts of the agricultural economy prospered but other parts did not. In particular export crops – pyrethrum, fruit, wheat – fell away and the sharp increase in the costs of fuel after 1973 accelerated the transformation of the Kenyan economy. From being – or seeming to be – a showpiece of conservative mixed economics it became cumbered with inflation, an adverse balance of payments and urban slums (Kenya has the highest population growth in Africa). An additional item on the debit side of the economy was the maltreatment of the Asian population which numbered 270,000 at independence, of whom all but 70,000 fled in the years that followed. By 1982, when that year's coup turned into a razzia against Asians, the survivors were fewer than 0.5 per cent of the population but still owned four-fifths of the retail trade and provided a quarter of GNP. (In the same year Milton Obote was trying to entice back to Uganda some of the 60,000 Asians expelled by Idi Amin ten years earlier.)

A third factor in the discontents of the early 1980s was the government's tilt towards the United States. This involvement arose out of the geopolitical strategies of the Indian Ocean (of which more in a later chapter), following the displacement of American by Soviet power in Ethiopia and the consequent American plan to turn Mombasa into a major American naval base. The development of the base provided work and profits but most of the profits went to white or largely white companies and in seeking an East African ally against the Soviet Union the Americans contributed to the latent instability within that chosen ally.

Although comparatively stable and comparatively prosperous within the circle of its neighbours, Kenya displays two of Africa's principal weaknesses: economic precariousness and ethnic conflict.

These place its future under the sign of uncertainty. Deterioration on either front is likely to affect the other, and simultaneous deterioration on both can quickly generate crisis.

III

The familiar categories of capitalist and socialist apply in Africa only with modifications. Kenya and Ivory Coast are examples of the capitalist way in Africa but are not replicas of the western model. Western capitalism draws, or tries to draw, a sharp line between the state and the private sector and deplores every encroachment by the former into the field of the latter. Even when closely linked in practice western statesmen and capitalists maintain this distinction between their activities even to the point of disposing of their personal share-holdings when they take public office. Africans do not follow this practice or accept the theory which prompts it. African capitalism functions within a system which admits – virtually of necessity – extensive and positive state intervention in the economy, thus producing a state capitalism which is the analogue of the state socialism prevalent in the communist world. The African capitalist statesman, like the Russian communist statesman, is an Erastian supremo in the mode of the European sovereign who, in the days when the main challenge to the state came from the church rather than the entrepreneurial bourgeoisie, set the state firmly above and in control of the church (first in Byzantium and later in the Protestant west). The outcome in Africa is a form of capitalism which, if it endures and the more it succeeds, will diverge increasingly from a western capitalism whose philosophical bedrock is a separation of political and economic powers. (The subordination of the state to a federation or association of states would not affect the thrust of this argument.)

African socialism has similarly to take into account an environment which modifies its extra-African heritage.

Socialism, as an ingredient in the intellectual hamper of African leaders, was subordinated to anti-colonialism so long as colonial rule persisted. But for some of these leaders – Julius Nyerere and Leopold Senghor are the clearest examples – socialism was an important element from the beginning, if only because the essential negativeness of anti-colonialism was in the long run intellectually unsatisfying. The main sources of this socialism were western European and Islamic: political leaders in British and French colonies became acquainted with mainstream socialist thinking of the nineteenth century and after, while their contemporaries in northern Africa (Nasser, Ben Bella) drew some of their ideas and aspirations from the radical teaching of the Syrian Baath and its antecedents. European socialism, however, could be adapted only with difficulty since African societies are overwhelmingly rural, whereas European socialism flourished within the Industrial Revolution. African socialists tended in consequence to hark back to the pre-industrial, cooperative socialism which inspired experiments like New Harmony and New Lanark. But the vagueness and romanticism of these ideas are not to everybody's taste and stronger fare was sought in a more 'scientific' socialism, also derived from Western Europe (the phrase is Engels') but developed in and associated with Eastern Europe under the no less vague denomination of Marxism-Leninism – a label adopted by Marian Ngouabe in Congo in 1964, Said Barre in Somalia in 1970, Matthieu Kerekou in Benin in 1974 and by the leaders of the more protracted and violent struggles in the Portuguese territories.

Chronologically the first challenge to the oligarchical conservativism exemplified in Ivory Coast and Kenya came in Guinea which, with its short-term partners in Ghana and Mali, represented in the late 1950s and early 1960s a radical anti-capitalism: radical in the sharpness of their anti-colonial reactions and anti-capitalist in protest against the spoliation of their domestic resources.

Yet this contrast has a misleading simplicity which must not be overstated. Beneath the skin all these countries were more akin than dissimilar. Guinea's initial course was not so much chosen as forced upon it, and Sekou Toure himself was a leader with many of the same personal antecedents, social and political, as Houphouet-Boigny. Although Guinea became notorious as a left-wing African state singled out for special cosseting by Moscow, this phase lasted only a few years and was followed by the renewal of links with France and participation in a new West African economic association dominated by Nigeria. In Ghana Nkrumah's course was not so much radical and left wing as unsteady. Ghana was the first black African member of the British Commonwealth and Nkrumah, although anti-American (largely as a result of the murder of his friend Lumumba), was not anti-British once British rule had been removed. Both Sekou Toure and Nkrumah exemplified an important shift in African attitudes towards the United States which, from being revered as the proponents of the Atlantic Charter and the world's most outspoken critic of colonial rule, became identified first with Africa's European overlords and then with multi-national exploitative capitalism.

Ghana became independent with exceptionally handsome reserves derived principally from the development of cocoa in the southwest corner of the colony of the Gold Coast from the beginning of the century. At independence Ghana was well ahead of its neighbours in growth rate, income per head, education and other indices of economic and social performance. Smaller than Ivory Coast but with a larger population, it was a manageable entity with a mixed agricultural and mineral base (gold, bauxite, manganese). As in Ivory Coast, the strongest element in its economy was a territorially limited, export-orientated agriculture which was considerably better financed and developed than the agriculture of the rest of the new state, particularly its northern areas which had been added by the British to their colony of the Gold Coast. Its leaders, including Kwame Nkrumah, belonged to a coastal middle class which was small in numbers but thrusting and well educated. Yet within two decades the Ghanaian economy was in ruins, the country had suffered four military coups, public services and educations were sliding towards calamity, opportunities for the younger generation had been destroyed and governments could no longer protect life, limb or property.

It has been common to blame this disaster on individuals, beginning with Nkrumah. There are always guilty men, or foolish ones. Nkrumah wasted Ghana's substance and his rule saw the beginnings of corruption which became both scandalous and burdensome. As his difficulties increased he resorted to the arrest or exile of opponents, preached a crazy ideology and established an incompetent dictatorship. He ran Ghana's reserves down from £200 million to £4 million and its external debt up to nearly £300 million. He was ousted in 1966 by the army (Colonel Ankrah), which gave way after three years to a new civilian regime under Dr Busia, who lasted less than three years before a second army coup (General Acheampong, 1972), which was followed by a coup within the armed forces (General Akuffo, 1978) and another of the same kind (Flight Lieutenant Rawlings, 1979), a return to civilian rule (1980) and the second coming of Flight Lieutenant Rawlings (1981).

All these permutations marked transfers of power within a comparatively narrow class, evidently incompetent in government. Neither civilians nor military knew what to do; alternatively, they knew what to do but lacked the power to get it done. The worsening situation was aggravated in 1979 when the first Rawlings coup was marked by the execution of a dozen leaders of the previous regime, a sinister precedent copied in the next year in Liberia.

Ghana's problems were overwhelmingly economic in the sense that other problems would have been easy to handle if the economic performance had been better. Opposition between the landed and merchant classes and the working classes led in Nkrumah's time to strikes but these could have been avoided if the workers' wages had not been cut in the face of economic decline. Trouble with immigrant workers (who entered the country when Ghana offered better prospects than its needy neighbours) led in 1970 to deportations under an Aliens Act which were necessitated by rising unemployment. Latent discontent in the traditionally neglected north and the racially distinct east was economically aggravated.

These economic failures condemned Ghana to stagnation and instability at home and to insignificance in the international community. But they were by no means entirely its own fault. The new men failed to provide government but outsiders contributed to Ghana's dismal history. Bauxite provides the cautionary tale.

Bauxite – so called from Les Baux in Provence where it was first identified – is a raw material which is the base of the modern aluminium industry which came into existence a hundred years ago with the discovery that bauxite can be made to yield alumina and these alumina can be turned into aluminium. Before these discoveries aluminium was a rarity. Bauxite is a composite clay which can be purified in such a way that the alumina are separated. These are in their turn separated from oxygen by electrolysis to produce aluminium. Because the raw bauxite is to be found in many parts of the world and because the aluminium industry is, by contrast, concentrated in four or five large corporations, economic power lies with the manufacturers and not the primary producers.

One consequence of this situation is that there is no world price for bauxite. The producer of bauxite has to sell to one of the international corporations which together form a cartel and dictate prices and levels of production. Furthermore, it lies in the manufacturers' power to decide whether the bauxite shall be turned into alumina at source by the producer or elsewhere by their own subsidiaries. If the manufacturers decree that they will buy bauxite but not alumina there is no point in the producer setting up an industry for purifying his bauxite and selling alumina. He must accept the (comparatively low) price offered for the bauxite and forgo the prospect of making money out of the initial manufacturing process as well as the mining of the raw material. In this way his profits are greatly limited.

Nkrumah's great Volta River dam was planned with the intention, among other things, of linking it with a smelter for the treatment of

Ghanaian bauxite. But this scheme miscarried. The dam was built by Ghana as part of a bargain with foreign (in this case American) interests which themselves built – and then wholly owned – the smelter. Ghana undertook to supply power from the dam to the smelter at cut prices and also granted various fiscal concessions. It failed, however, to include in the contract any provision requiring the owners of the smelter to buy Ghanaian bauxite; and these owners, having secured a cheaply operated smelter, imported bauxite from elsewhere. So Ghana sold less bauxite than anticipated and was committed to selling a substantial volume of the electricity generated by its dam at an artificially low price. Ghana made a bad bargain for which, in strictly commercial terms, its inexperience and poor economic clout were to blame – but which, in wider terms, was seen as a piece of sharp practice by foreign capitalists.

The moral of this story is not to point the finger of accusation at western capitalists. Capitalists do not pretend to be moral: they have other values. They aim to be efficient and disclaim the incursion of moral values into business. But the other side of the picture – particularly in the case of a powerful corporation which a weak new state cannot easily tax – shows foreign capitalists doing more harm than good. The new state is resentfully forced or innocently induced into a bargain which is by common-sense standards manifestly unfair.

Western capitalists are not the only offenders. In Guinea the exploiter was the state capitalism of the Soviet Union. The result was much the same.

Guinea possesses one-third of the world's bauxite. With, in addition, iron ores, uranium, gold, diamonds, offshore oil and three major rivers it is potentially a rich country. Yet by 1980 its GNP amounted to about £2 per head per week. Its mineral resources, like much of its fertile farming land, are barely exploited and in no area has it developed the economic strength to strike good bargains with foreign customers. At independence Sekou Toure turned to the Soviet Union, if only in default of anywhere else to look. The Russians agreed to develop the bauxite round Kindia and set up a company to do so which, theoretically, was a joint Russo-Guinean enterprise but, in practice, was entirely run by Russians: even the lorry drivers came from the Soviet Union.

The Russians set an arbitrary price of $6 a tonne for the bauxite up to 1976 when they raised it to $16, still a low price by any calculation. They credited the proceeds to a clearing account and debited Guinea with the cost of arms and other supplies, also at arbitrary figures. This mean and impolitic juggling with the figures contributed to the rapid breach in Russo-Guinean relations to which we will revert when we come to consider the USSR's record in post-independence Africa. It also persuaded Africans everywhere that the outside world – communist as well as western – was interested in Africa only for what it could get out of it and, consequently, had an interest in keeping it economically impotent. But the problem of how to become stronger without outside help remained.

In Guinea's case the answer, or part-answer, was to veer back towards France. The Ghana–Guinea–Mali union showed that ideology was no help in economic affairs. Guinea had every reason to turn in 1958 to Moscow and as much reason to turn away again a few years later. When in 1974 Benin declared itself a Marxist-Leninist state it did not leave the French economic zone; and when Mozambique became the only African member of Comecon it was clear that this was a political gesture without economic stuffing.

IV

Self-help is perennially heart-warming; communal self-help doubly so. But it is not thereby also successful. Examples of societies or countries which have contrived their own industrial development are few and far between. There has to be a first starter and it happened to be Britain but as the industrial revolution spread the capital and techniques which powered it were most often borrowed from abroad: the first stages of the industrial development of the United States, for example, were financed by British capital. Twentieth century Africa has (with the possible exception of South Africa) no chance whatever of substantial economic transformation by its own unaided efforts.

Self-help is not the same as self-sufficiency. Self-help is active, self-sufficiency passive. A self-sufficient society wishes to remain what it is. It eschews outside contacts on the grounds that, whatever their benefits, they entail greater disadvantages – the disturbance, for example, of a settled and traditional way of life which suits that society and its values. This attitude may be more romantic than anything else, specially in the eyes of the outside beholder, but it exists and commands respect. But it does not exist in Africa where societies, however wary of foreign incursion, do not want to stand still.

Or do they? Most African societies are overwhelmingly rural and therefore conservative, which is to say that they want to stand still while nevertheless having the benefits of not doing so. This therefore is a second dilemma for political leaders in these countries. On the one hand foreign money and skills are needed for progress but foreign involvement is tainted by colonialism and capitalism. On the other hand the bulk of the population consists of a peasantry which, temperamentally and all over the world, presents a stolid obstacle to change, however moderate and sensible.

Julius Nyerere of Tanzania faced both these dilemmas at once. Tanzania is comparatively homogeneous, with a common language and no major tribal conflicts, but it is also one of Africa's least well endowed countries. About twice the size of Kenya and four times as big as Uganda it is however the poor relation in East Africa and so markedly dependent on external assistance and regional cooperation. Its origins were turbulent and unprecedented since it was formed in 1964 by the merger of Tanganyika and Zanzibar (two territories ceded by Germany, the one in 1919 as a consequence of defeat in the First World War and the other in 1890 as a swap for Heligoland). Tanganyika became independent at the end of 1961 after nearly half a century of British tutelage under League of Nations mandate and United Nations trusteeship; Zanzibar in 1963. Their merger in the next year was the unpremeditated consequence of Britain's transfer of power in Zanzibar to a largely alien Arab minority representing no more than a fifth of the population.

A few months later a motley anti-Arab union overthrew the new regime. Among its leaders were some alleged to have Chinese or Cuban connections. The situation was obscure and alarming and under nobody's control, so that the despatch of a small squad of police by Nyerere in effect annexed the smaller state to the larger. This merger was, however, doubly embarrassing for Nyerere. His new Zanzibari associates included clownish bravos and ruthless autocrats who consorted ill with one of Africa's most sophisticated and fastidious leaders. In addition, if haphazardly, the fracas in Zanzibar coincided almost to the day with mutinies (over pay and promotion) in the Tanganyikan army which weakened and humiliated Nyerere's government, the more so since they were brought under control with the assistance of British troops despatched from Kenya. (There were similar disturbances in the same week in Kenya itself and in Uganda.) These episodes proved ephemeral: Nyerere overrode the embarrassments caused him by the merger with Zanzibar, while the mutinies posed no more than a momentary threat to his position in Tanganyika itself. Twenty years later he, alone among the first generation of East African statesmen, was still head of his state and the longest serving statesman in the whole of Africa with the sole exception of

Houphouet-Boigny. Yet during those years Tanzania became progressively poorer and unhappier, its natural economic deprivation accentuated by its determination to turn in on itself, by the collapse of the projected East African Federation and by the failure of its internal social experiments.

For Nyerere – as for Mao whom Nyerere admired – self-help seemed the sure road to betterment, and self-help in Tanzania meant inevitably putting the emphasis on farming and not on manufacture. Like many African leaders Nyerere is a socialist. In Africa as elsewhere, socialism is a very broad term. For Africans independence entailed considerable changes and for African socialists these changes should extend to two things in particular, both of which require action by the state: first, redistribution of private wealth in the direction of greater equality, including the provision of social services and security for the poor; and, secondly, modernization of methods of production, not excluding public or communal ownership of the means and processes of production. Proponents of such changes want to achieve them by democratic and legislative roads but are not always opposed to their introduction. Proponents of such changes want to achieve them by democratic and legislative roads but are not always opposed to their introduction by military or other authoritarian fiat or by violence. They give a high, perhaps overriding, priority to the reconstruction of the societies and economies which they have inherited from the colonial past and are sceptical about any partnership with foreign capital which, when it finds indigenous associates, does little more than exalt and corrupt a selfish elite and so increase inequality and debase standards. African socialists therefore are hostile to foreign capital on pragmatic as well as dogmatic grounds.

Nyerere in addition is a believer in the virtues and efficacy of a devolved, grass-roots democracy. He planned therefore a peaceful, disciplined, austere, socialist, rural revolution within a one-party state dominated by a democratically organized party which would direct and teach. The Arusha Declaration of 1967, followed two years later by the first *ujmaa* programme, aimed to increase agricultural production by grouping homesteads in communal development areas. As it proceeded the *ujmaa* experiment proposed to sort out and resettle nine-tenths of the rural population and did in fact reorganize two-thirds of it – a killing pace which achieved more resettlement than production (reminiscent of the craze during Mao's Cultural Revolution for making steel in backyards, a campaign which produced a fair amount of steel but little of it any good). Like similar schemes the *ujmaa* experiment depended for its dynamism on the belief that

47

collaborative effort brings happiness and profits, but it was handi-capped by the fact that this belief needed to be inculcated from outside into peasants with a stubborn individualism, little education and no ideology.

The ultimate aim was a greater degree of economic independence by means of radical changes in the rural economy. The experiment failed. It drove a wedge between the ruling elite and the mass of a peasantry which was not ready for such change and reacted, some-times with violence, against being told by townees how to work the land. As in so many parts of the world the conservatism of the peasants defeated the good intentions and superior logic of the reformers. Nor were the latter always patient. When faced with the peasant's refusal to be argued out of his rut they tried to kick him out of it. This drive was all the more unsuccessful since it coincided with shortages which confirmed the peasant in his belief that he knew better. So far as he could see the only gainers from rural socialism and modernization were the richer peasants, the kulaks, who were for him a class apart and whose fortunes were no guide to his own best interests.

Bureaucratic muddle and poor services contributed to a decline in productivity per head which was aggravated when the peasant was moved into *ujmaa* villages situated hours away from his land. Ineffi-cient managements under government or party supervision incurred losses which were settled by inflationary government hand-outs. Prices rose; price controls did not work; shortages and black markets appeared; inflation, corruption and unemployment spread. So far from winning economic independence Tanzania remained excep-tionally dependent on foreign aid. Workers' strikes and student pro-tests met with strong-arm responses. The despatch in 1979 of 10,000 troops to Uganda with the laudable mission of overthrowing Idi Amin was a heavy expense; they returned to a country with no work for the demobilized. Authority disintegrated and at the end of 1982 there was at least one (abortive) coup against Nyerere.

There is another side to this story. The leader who eschews outside aid and contacts is particularly vulnerable to criticism. When his experiments go wrong he can hardly blame those whom he has kept out. And yet to some extent he can and Tanzania is as much entitled as any state to claim that, for reasons beyond its control, the 1970s were unluckily intemperate. The post-1973 oil crisis, worldwide economic recession and a series of unnaturally severe droughts played a big part in Tanzania's misfortunes, and since areas outside the *ujmaa* schemes fared neither worse nor better than *ujmaa* complexes – and the towns as badly as the countryside – the government was able to conclude that the main fault lay with neither the theory nor the practice of its rural socialism. Yet after nearly twenty years of independence Tanzania, having eschewed industrialization and concentrated on the development of what it has, was virtually bankrupt. Nyerere conducted the state entirely differently from Nkrumah in Ghana, not to mention Mobutu in Zaire, but in one central respect the result was the same: his rule has not been justified by performance. Tanzania remains a hard, harsh place to live in – and is becoming more difficult to govern.

Yet in another respect the result is different. Even if Nyerere's socialist programme has been a failure – in the sense of failing to satisfy the material expectations of independence – and even if Tanzania's single party TANU (later CCM: Chama Cha Mapinduzi) has forfeited much of its initial popularity, Nyerere himself retains respect at home and abroad. (A similar situation has developed in Zambia with regard to Kenneth Kaunda and his party UNIP.) Tanzania's miserable economic record has escaped the worst of the scandals and corruption which have besmirched economic growth in the pre-eminent capitalist states, Kenya and Ivory Coast, Zaire and Nigeria. It may be a moot point whether the comparative honesty of socialist states is due to their socialist ideals or to the poverty which makes them barren ground for corruption. But however that may be, Tanzania has so far retained in failure a dignity achieved in few other African states. How much consolation that brings to its disappointed and hungry underdogs and its increasingly restless army is not a question open to assessment. Nevertheless Tanzania broached the 1980s with a better prospect than most African states for achieving gradually and peaceably the approaching transition from the first generation of self-rule to the next.

5 THE REGIONAL ESCAPE

I

The political and economic shortcomings surveyed in the foregoing chapters prey upon one another. The weaker the government, the poorer its performance and vice versa and so on in a spiral whose descent is increasingly difficult to stop. Additional and blatant failures, such as corruption and urban violence, cluster round this central disaster. While there is no easy way out there are two necessary preconditions: the first is to reassert the primacy of agriculture and communications in the economic picture and the second is to recognize the inadequacy of most of the new states as agents of political stability and economic progress. What should then emerge, and are perhaps beginning to emerge, are regional associations or unions of states pooling their resources with the primary purposes of building roads, financing modern farming and training men and women to work and understand the land. Giving priority to such measures would have been sensible at any point in the short history of independent Africa. By now it is not only sensible but urgent since many African governments are courting bankruptcy, anarchy and even revolution.

Even more compelling is the shift from expansion to survival. New policies and new institutions are needed not in order to pursue the aims of the 1960s and 1970s – namely, industrial innovation – but in order to maintain living standards and fend off famine. Food has become the prime concern as even basic foods have become unprocurable in one place after another. In the 1960s Africa overall was not far short of self-sufficiency in food. But in the same decade food production per head of population declined 6–7 per cent. In the 1970s, when the population increased by nearly 40 per cent, it declined at least twice as fast, and by 1980 Africa was importing a fifth of its food.

African populations were growing faster than any others in the world. Growth rates over 3 per cent a year were common. (Kenya exceeded 4 per cent; in Europe 1 per cent was exceptional.) Populations were doubling in a generation. The main reason was the falling death rate at both ends of life, bringing with it a relative decline in the proportion of men and women of working age. Contraceptive advice and services were in general rudimentary. Urban populations grew much faster than the average: Africa's main cities were growing at about 10 per cent a year.

There is nothing unnatural about a demographic increase of this order. What is distinctive about Africa today is the absence of checks on natural increase. Malthus wrote: 'It may be safely asserted . . . that population, where unchecked, increases in a geometric progression of such a nature as to double itself every twenty-five years'. Malthus was a mathematician and knew what he was talking about. He also wrote that such increases were rare because they were normally checked (except, according to his observation, in the United States of America of his day). What the checks are is the main subject of his famous essays on population which were inspired by his conviction that populations must increase faster than the stuff of subsistence if both processes are left to natural increase. In fact his conviction was mistaken, not because he was wrong about populations but because he underrated man's capacity to expand food production. But his central concern with human health and happiness remains sound if and where food production is not increased *pari passu* with the population – and this has been occurring in Africa.

The problem of food has been aggravated by fearful droughts, and even in areas where the cultivated acreage increased yields often fell. In consequence food consumption per head fell by 10 per cent during the 1970s, in spite of doubled imports of grain. The consequences were manifest in starvation, migration and debt, as population growth outstripped resources.

Rural decline started a chain of ills: a flight, principally of men, to the towns or their outskirts; overcrowding, disease, unemployment and crime; less home-grown food and so more expensive food with therefore an upward spiral in the import bill and a downward spiral in health. All over Africa the neglect or mismanagement of agriculture created fevered proletariats which did not previously exist, had no hope of a decent life except possibly through revolution, and from being society's prime producers had been transformed into producing nothing but squalor.

The failure of the land to feed the towns is a vicious spiral, familiar above all from the example of the USSR where, for over half a century, no government has succeeded either in cajoling or in coercing the peasant into producing an adequate marketable surplus. The main cause is the government's refusal to pay him enough to make it worth his while to do so. By keeping prices low in the interests of the urban consumer governments create a dearth, since the peasant's retort to a cheap food policy is to produce enough for himself and his family but no more. Peasant power is negative and frequently ineffectual but the barely conscious reaction of the peasantry can have a powerful effect on the way the national economy goes.

Next to the servicing of unwieldy foreign debts, food imports were the severest burden on the balance of payments of African countries, many of which had previously exported food. In Zaire, for example, where before independence food accounted for nearly half the value of exports, farms were untended, food was imported at considerable cost – and the average expectation of life in this country of fabulous potential wealth was 40. Other examples from Ghana and Kenya have already been cited. In Zimbabwe, by contrast, in 1981 the prices offered to farmers were raised and record crops were produced.

The political consequences of misery can be neither quantified nor foretold with any precision, but there are few things more disruptive of a society than a rising population unmatched by commensurate economic growth. It confronts the haves with the need to deny the expectations, even to depress the living standards, of the have-nots in order to defend their own way of life and satisfy their own minimum requirements. The comparatively prosperous minority foresees no way of retaining its enviable state – let alone improving it – without denying to the majority the material progress to which it looks forward and to which it considers itself entitled. Government becomes therefore factional, ungenerous and repressive.

Historians of eighteenth century England have plausibly conjectured that the repressive legislation imposed in that age by the ruling propertied class was occasioned, in significant part, by the consciousness that the population had begun to take off. It nearly doubled between 1700 and 1800, and this increase would have been even steeper but for a conditioning factor which appears to be peculiar to pre-industrial and early industrial societies in Europe – namely, a predisposition to comparatively late marriage, a cultural phenomenon (not present in modern Africa) reflecting the view that the ability to set up house independently is a prerequisite of marriage. However that may be, the swelling population of England scared the minority which, quite apart from being outnumbered, feared the supposedly brutish, violent and amoral nature of the masses and by attempting to keep them in their place exacerbated the very threat which it feared. In the next century population growth was tempered by increasing wealth and by emigration.

Rulers are seldom wholly malevolent but their concern for the ruled fluctuates with their own well-being. Two hundred years later the genuine enthusiasm to be found in all classes in Britain for the welfare state became dowsed among the better-off when they discovered how much the social services were cutting into their personal amenities and budgets – that the lessening of inequalities entailed an unexpected or unacceptable degree of sacrifice by themselves.

This dilemma is far more acute in Africa. In twentieth century Britain the economy might be static, but so was the population. In Africa the population was not only rising at an unprecedented rate in sluggish or stagnant economies but was being re-shaped so that the unproductive young and old were increasing in proportion to those of working age. One likely consequence is repression to, perhaps beyond, the point of popular revolt and the increasing dependence of government on the police, secret intelligence and armed force.

Latin America holds up a mirror to this situation. Independent for a century and a half the countries of South and Central America – some poor, some rich, a few exceedingly poor or rich – are almost without exception unstable and the root of this instability is the revolt of the many against the few, a challenge to the established position of a small ruling class made prosperous by agriculture or minerals and supported by a military caste of similar social origins or aspirations. This rule has been threatened or displaced in a variety of ways: by revolution (Bolivia), by a populist movement (Peronism in Argentina), by a discontented wing of the army (Peru) or by a combination of such forces. The enemies of the established order range from the violently indignant to staider elements rendered uneasy by calculation or by conscience. Their common aim, whether or not they make common cause, is a redistribution of political power.

Seen from outside this conflict has often looked different. The war of the haves against the have-nots has been reinterpreted as one between left and right in which the left consciously or unconsciously lends itself to a global conspiracy to help the Soviet Union to defeat the United States. Latin American have-nots – largely peasants who, however incensed against the ruling oligarchy, are no more left wing than peasants anywhere else – have no inkling of this alleged conspiracy. All they see of the outside world, if anything, is that their mighty American neighbour to the north is apparently on the side of the oligarchs and autocrats who oppress them.

Yet the myth has enough substance to make it effective. Anti-government forces are, in conventional political jargon, left wing. They are not only prepared to use violence but frequently have nothing else to use; and they are willing to accept help, particularly weapons, from anywhere – which in practice leads them to communist scources such as Cuba and so indirectly the USSR, since western countries are more likely to be arming their enemies. Among the leaders most are merely seeking support where they can find it; some are also ideologists with a belief in socialism of one kind or another (Comte, Marx, Lenin, Trotsky and others); a very few may be committed politicians with a burning desire to see the USSR triumph over the United States.

The principal difference between these countries and Africa, apart from their much longer span of independent statehood, is their proximity to the United States which makes them sensitive targets for intervention by Washington and likewise by Moscow. But if geographically the cases differ, politically African states have been going the way of Latin America, fostering within themselves a turbulence liable to be interpreted by outsiders in global terms of superpower conflict. Africa therefore is not merely a political and economic mess. It is courting external interference in its affairs, deriving from outsiders' misinterpretation of those affairs. The African state, like the Latin American state, becomes incapable of adjusting its social and economic tensions without turning into one more piece in the superpower line-up, and when this happens both superpowers feel justified in paying scant attention to its sovereignty. Some states will fare better than others. Even a superpower will not handle Nigeria or Zaire or Algeria – large and well endowed even when ill managed – like banana republics. But the smaller fry are reduced to flotsam and jetsam of the international system – so long, at least, as each tries to stand alone.

II

Politically, independent Africa is at present committed to fragmentation. African unity, like the Arab unity institutionalized in the Arab League, has been unable to counter or even temper the conquest of the continent by the vogue for the sovereign state. By 1980 the OAU comprised fifty independent states on the continent or within reasonable reach of its shores (in the Atlantic and Pacific oceans). Economically, however, there were hankerings for something larger and more effective than most of these sovereign states and so attempts to create regional economic associations compatible with national sovereignties – an endeavour essentially similar to the creation in Europe of the European Economic Community, a political sport born of economic necessity.

The OAU itself offers its members no economic salvation. Its twenty-year record is fairly dismal. It possesses no independent resources and has failed to promote even such basic necessities as the road or rail networks which Africa urgently needs or any common financial or commercial services. Although by its existence it continues to embody the ideal of African unity, its activities have done little to gild that ideal. It has been embarrassingly incompetent to do anything about the shameful regimes of Idi Amin in Uganda or Jean-Bedel Bokassa in the Central African Republic or Francisco Macias Nguema in Equatorial Guinea. Even in its pre-eminent political field it has made no dent in *apartheid* in South Africa and contributed, as an organization, nothing to the dramas of Zimbabwean or Namibian liberation. Although some of these matters lie, strictly speaking, outside its terms of reference its limited impact is evidently due to incapacity rather than deliberate choice, and in 1982 its dwindling repute was further eroded when it was twice forced to cancel its annual conference due to be held in Tripoli.

The first cancellation was caused by a split in the membership over the status of the Polisario guerrillas who claimed recognition as the Sahrawi Arab Democratic Republic. Polisario – Popular Front for the Liberation of Sanguiet el-Hamra and Rio de Oro – had the support of twenty-seven OAU members and of its Secretary General (who was however disowned by his own government). This group, a majority but not the two thirds required for a quorum, maintained that they were following the OAU's fundamental rule that colonial frontiers, however illogical or inconvenient, must be preserved in the post-colonial age for fear of otherwise unleashing ethnic or religious conflicts all over the continent; they and the Polisario were asserting the separateness, within (roughly) its old Spanish borders, of what had been Rio de Oro, in opposition to Morocco which had hoped to acquire most of it.

The second cancellation arose out of dissension over whether to accept Hissen Habre or Goukouni Oueddei as legitimate head of state in Chad. The OAU was weakened not only because it could find no way to settle these quarrels but also because the first of them threatened by its very nature to open the Pandora's box of territorial disputes that the OAU was committed to containing.

Constitutionally the OAU's existence was no bar to the formation of regional associations, and federal notions had been around in Africa for a long time. Both France and Britain toyed with them. France brigaded its West African colonies and its Equatorial ones into federations and Britain took the first steps towards an East African Federation.

The French federations did not survive independence but split up in much the same way as Central America split up after severance from Spain in 1821. There were some limited functional survivals: the Chad Convention, the Niger River Convention, the Senegal River Convention (there was also a Mano River Convention between Liberia and Sierra Leone), and of wider import OAMCE (Organization for Economic Cooperation in Africa and Madagascar: 1961). This last body, whose main purpose was to convert pre-independence economic relations with France into a post-independence mould, was expanded in 1965 by the addition of ex-Belgian Zaire: loose ends of colonialism re-tied in a new pattern.

British territories in West Africa were more scattered than French – none touched another – but in the east the Kenya and Uganda protectorates, established at the turn of the century, adjoined one another and both marched with Tanganyika which came under British administration by the mandate agreement of 1919. The beginnings of an East African Federation were laid with a joint currency board (1905), a postal union (1911) and a customs union (1917), followed by the East African High Commission (1948) and the East Africa Common Service Organization (1961). After the liberation of all three territories the Kampala Agreement of 1964 and the East Africa Cooperation Treaty of 1967 tried to keep the cooperative spirit alive but it gradually faded away. Capitalist Kenya and socialist Tanganyika distrusted one another. Joint rail and air services were mismanaged. Amin's rule in Uganda and the collapse of the Ugandan economy were a final blow.

Two other initiatives were more promising. In West Africa sixteen states created in 1975, at the instance of Nigeria and Togo, the Economic Organization of West African States (ECOWAS) dedicated to free trade, a common market and joint enterprises. The members also signed a non-aggression pact. In 1979 nine states created a similar Southern African Development Coordinating Conference (SADCC), a standing body with a permanent secretariat and institutions. Both these organizations recognized the prior demands of communications, agriculture and education and both accepted the need for foreign capital and skills. But although superficially akin these two ventures in cooperation were also very different.

One main difference was due to the presence of Nigeria in ECOWAS. With a population about equal to that of all the members of SADCC put together Nigeria overshadowed ECOWAS geographically and demographically and, with the sudden access of huge oil revenues, became in the 1970s an economic giant too. Consequently Nigeria was as much patron as partner in ECOWAS, playing a role for which SADCC had no candidate. This role moreover was determined by a single and, as it turned out, variable factor: the flow and world price of oil.

Nigeria, *sui generis* in Africa, represents both distortion and hope. The discovery of oil placed it in a new category of state – the cash-flow state. So long as the demand for oil and its price remained high the cash was superabundant. It swamped the country's other economic assets and activities, lifted its economy on to a different plane, dominated its development plans, offered a salve for internal divisions, turned Nigeria into a neighbour not only powerful and populous but also possibly bountiful, and gave it new weight throughout the whole of Africa and beyond. Great opportunities were opened for both altruism and greed.

By 1980 oil accounted for 93 per cent of Nigeria's foreign earnings and 80 per cent of government income; oil income reached $20 billion a year. Nigeria had leaped at a bound into the top six of the world's oil exporters, projecting the production of over 2 million barrels of high priced light oil a day – of which only a tenth was required for domestic use. On this basis oil would pay for agricultural and industrial development, dispensing with the need to choose between the two; it would make the country self-sufficient in basic foods by the mid-1980s and would at the same time create new industries to magnify export earnings and build up domestic investment capital. There would also be more than a little left over to help friends and neighbours.

These exciting visions had to be modified, at least temporarily, by circumstances which reminded Nigerians that wealth of this kind depended on uncontrollable events in the outside world. Nigeria was a beneficiary of the big rises in oil prices effected by OPEC from 1973 onwards – that is to say, by the politico-economic power of a mainly Middle Eastern cartel taking advantage of a sellers' market. But Nigerian oil came into the market in the same period as Alaskan and North Sea oil and a few years later the combined effects of price rises and world recession depressed the market and obliged Nigeria to limit its production and reduce its price. Daily output fell below 1 million barrels and then lower and two-thirds of the country's accumulated reserves of $9 billion had to be spent. Although a new plan for 1981–85 projected a second boom with annual growth of 8 per cent or more, the mischances and exuberance of the first boom had taken some of the financial gilt off the economic gingerbread. Ironically oil turned Nigeria into something like a one-crop economy since oil revenues led not only to a complete recasting of the economic future but also to the adoption of plans wholly dependent on oil.

These gyrations affected Nigeria's equipoise at a time when civilians were resuming control after thirteen years of civil war and military rule. Nigeria had a record of instability and violence which wealth might temper but fluctuations in wealth might revive and exacerbate. It was regarded in West Africa with apprehension as well as envy for if it were true that economic progress required regional cooperation, Nigeria's own prosperity and stability were fundamental to the fortunes of a dozen or more states from Senegal to Cameroon.

Nigeria was one of colonialism's more artificial creations, completed when Britain in 1914 joined its two colonies of Lagos and Southern Nigeria with the northern principalities or emirates over which it established control around 1900. The resulting amalgam of languages, religions and social systems was held together by British power until independence in 1960 when the new state was born with three (later four) main blocks or provinces balancing one another in a federal parliamentary political framework. Distrust proving stronger than constitutional cement, civil war broke out in 1966. Its outcome was the defeat of the attempted secession of the Ibos of eastern Nigeria and a corresponding victory for the principle of integration; the federation was preserved intact together with its innate stresses and strains. These were kept in check so long as politics were blanketed by successive military regimes (under Generals Yakubu Gowon, Murtala Mohammed and Olesegun Obasanjo) which tried also to defuse the country's internal animosities by constitutional reforms. The four large provinces were replaced by nineteen smaller states and in 1979 the military retired into the background after organizing and supervising orderly elections. Three years later further elections were held, this time under civilian supervision, but the sweeping victories of President Shagari's party transgressed credibility and reopened a prospect of civil strife. But memories of the war of the 1960s militated against its renewal, as did new opportunities for making money and the determination of the army (swollen from 10,000 to 150,000) to maintain the unity of the state in spite of its deep political, cultural and religious divisions. Trying to hold Nigeria together was like pretending that medieval Europe constituted a natural political entity called Christendom. Yet this centrifugal country was cast for the role of coordinating ECOWAS.

SADCC, by contrast, contained no such partner. But it has an overpowering neighbour. In purely economic terms SADCC should have embraced South Africa but in fact SADCC was created as a counterpoise to the economic power of South Africa and in response to South African schemes for a 'constellation' of states in the southern cone which was rejected by the rest of the region on political, not economic, grounds: South Africa's repulsive social and constitutional system. The preponderant economic power in southern Africa lay therefore on the fringes of SADCC and not within it, and since this economic power was matched by a no less preponderant military power SADCC was constantly exposed to such subversive tactics as South Africa might choose to adopt against any of its members.

The most promising among SADCC's separate economies was in Zimbabwe where a healthy agriculture was allied with an unusual diversity of mineral resources – copper, nickel, chrome, gold, asbestos. But no sooner did Zimbabwe attain its belated independence in 1980 than it was afflicted by a slump in the world prices of its principal exports and the demand for them. As export earnings fell and imports rose projected growth rates – 8 per cent a year in the domestic economy and 90 per cent over three years in export revenues – became visionary, thus compounding the country's internal problems (postwar recovery, tribal conflict, the conversion of guerrillas into farmers and sporadic drought) and weakening its position as the lynchpin of SADCC. Even more threatening to Zimbabwe and its partners in SADCC was the ability of a hostile South Africa to play cat and mouse with them

III

The attempt by South Africa's white minority to maintain its political and economic supremacy and to do so by *apartheid* has imposed on all southern Africa a pervasive uncertainty and instability.

The white minority in South Africa is a democracy which refuses to extend democracy to blacks. It also refuses them any professional, industrial or other employment above levels which, although they may shift upwards from time to time, are a standing barrier to black advancement. The white minority is therefore inextricably committed to racialism, since it can maintain its positions only by racial discrimination based on the theory and practice of inherent white superiority.

Not only is this doctrine repugnant to all non-whites and very many whites; it has been implemented by the Nationalist Party, which has been in power in South Africa since 1948, by over 300 statutes and by ruthless cruelty exercised through a police force licensed to use violence and torture as instruments of state policy. The world has had and still has a number of governments whose practices are as nauseating as those of South Africa, but few of them have openly made racism a primary intellectual tenet and political cornerstone, and this additional offence gives the South African problem a peculiar intractability. For non-whites – in particular Africans – South African *apartheid* is the devil with whom one may not compromise; for white South Africans themselves, or a substantial majority of them, their misdeeds beget further misdeeds which they can justify to their consciences only by branding their victims as submen or communist or terrorist devils with whom likewise it is unholy to parley.

The conviction of superiority which is at the base of *apartheid* is buttressed by confidence in white South Africa's military power and economic wealth. South Africa has fabulous natural resources and advanced technical skills, civil and military. It may possess nuclear weapons and certainly knows how to make them. During the 1970s, when it was virtually ostracized by most of the world and in danger of losing even its British and American friends, it demonstrated its strength by closing its most serious economic gap: it made itself independent of foreign fuels by developing its own plants for getting oil from coal.

South Africa believes furthermore that its wealth and its strategic position on the map make it indispensable to the western world in the conflict against Soviet communism. By one of nature's most striking geopolitical accidents South Africa contains a large proportion of the world's known reserves of crucial minerals, and this bargaining counter is reinforced in those cases where substantial quantities of these minerals outside South Africa are in the USSR and so obtainable only by Moscow's grace. Thus South Africa possesses 86 per cent of the world's known platinum ores (USSR 13 per cent); 83 per cent of chromes; 64 per cent of vanadium (USSR 33 per cent); 49 per cent of gold (USSR 19 per cent); 48 per cent of manganese (USSR 45 per cent); 46 per cent of fluorspar; 17 per cent of uranium (USSR 13 per cent).

There is also South Africa's proximity to one of the world's main sea routes. The passage from the Persian Gulf to New York via the Cape of Good Hope is 5,000 miles shorter than the alternative east-about route. It is used for nearly 1,000 tanker-journeys a year and carries three-quarters of Nato's oil and other strategic materials and up to 90 per cent of the oil imported by Europe's Nato members.

Yet the 1970s brought also doubts. The accelerating development of South Africa's resources and skills was unattainable without foreign capital and black labour. Capital, although it continued to flow in, was liable to dwindle if domestic political troubles increased. Even more problematic was the government's future control over a black labour force which was increasingly necessary (at ever higher levels of skill) and increasingly politicized. The demographic and economic absurdities of *apartheid* as applied in the bantustans or homelands became more and more evident. The collapse of Portuguese rule in southern Africa in 1974, followed by the defeat of the whites in Rhodesia and the looming necessity to let Namibia go, brought the enemy to the door; while in the same period such episodes as the riots in Soweto in 1976, the vigour of the international outcry over the murder of Steve Biko by the police in 1977, and splits and scandals within the Nationalist Party in 1978 fostered uneasiness in a white community which, however insensitive when it could comfortably turn its back to the real world, was also intelligent enough to realize when it must turn round and face facts.

The main fact is the threat to undiluted white power. The 1970s showed that this could not be taken for granted for ever. Although white power remains exceedingly difficult to assail, its eventual downfall is no longer unthinkable. So two problems arise: first, whether and how far to curtail it and, second, how to defend it for so long as this may be necessary.

The first question entails the partial abdication (no white thinks of total abdication) of an aristocracy of a special kind, an aristocracy based on colour and therefore far more offensive to its subordinates, and far more tenacious of its privileges, than any normal ruling class: South Africa's ruling class has no blurred edges. Many schemes have been mooted but none seems remotely acceptable to both sides. These schemes are broadly of two kinds: partition and power-sharing. Partition – the cession of part of the state to make a new black state – runs up against the whites' refusal to abandon the wealthier regions or to limit themselves to an area in any way commensurate with their relatively small numbers. Any plan which ensures them the space and wealth which they require is bound to leave the blacks overcrowded, impecunious and dependent still on migrating to white territory for wages and sustenance. Power-sharing remains a tabu if it involves releasing to blacks any capacity to overrule whites on any except trivial issues. Elaborating on previous ideas P. W. Botha, after becoming Prime Minister in 1978, propounded a plan for associating Indians and Coloureds with the whites in a new constitution but the blacks were simply left out, white supremacy was not imperilled and the Indians and Coloureds were suspicious of a scheme so evidently devised to divide them from the blacks. The best that could be said by the beginning of the 1980s was that a negotiation had begun with the Indians and Coloureds; that this process might be intended to lead to a negotiation with the blacks also; and that these negotiations might embrace matters of substance (particularly political power) and proceed fast enough to forestall the onset of violence as the normal and determining political mode of the country.

If white power, however trimmed, is to be maintained it must be actively defended. The Soweto riots were a shock because they showed the menacing face of internal insurrection. The power and ruthlessness of the police sufficed to master such upheavals but recurrent riots, besides stretching the resources of the dominant minority and damaging its economy, are bound to sap morale. They are moreover only half the problem, the other half being the vulnerability of the frontiers to guerrilla infiltration and subversion.

South Africa is confident of its power to defeat any attack by black states which is not openly and massively assisted by a non-African power – meaning the USSR (but this is an unlikely eventuality and one which can be counted on to bring other outside powers to the aid of the whites). There are some attendant worries: rising defence costs as a proportion of GNP, long land and sea frontiers, recruiting problems particularly of junior officers and senior NCOs, dependence on foreign sources for some parts of the armoury. But more worrying than these ancillary matters is the prospect of a wearing guerrilla campaign which the South African police and army could no doubt contain but could never bring to an end. Guerrilla fighters can expect havens in neighbouring black states which will also give them money, arms and training. These states have therefore to be regarded as to some degree hostile to South Africa. In reverse, they can not avoid importing into their affairs the extra strains and instability inseparable from giving aid and comfort to the enemies of a powerful neighbour.

One South African answer to the problem, considered in varying forms by all Prime Ministers from Smuts to Botha, is a zone or constellation of states brought into association by mutual economic needs and interests – and inevitably dominated by South Africa's vastly superior economy. South Africa's accords with Botswana, Lesotho, Swaziland and Malawi provide the pattern.

The first three of these states are more or less accidental abutments or enclaves whose special position in the structure of British power in southern Africa (as 'protectorates') was converted into political independence, the first two in 1966 and Swaziland in 1968. Economically they are hostages to South Africa and recognized to have exceptionally limited choices in the conduct of their affairs. Malawi is a somewhat different case, also economically beholden to South Africa but a more willing hostage so long as Hastings Banda rules. Autocratic, conservative and as moralistic in his way as a stern Boer pastor, Banda had been fiercely anti-British but subordinated his hatred of *apartheid* to his country's economic stringencies. Brooking no opposition at home he secured a kind of order together with steady economic growth which quintupled Malawi's GNP between independence in 1964 and 1980. Such results still much criticism.

So long as South Africa's neighbours were, with these four minor exceptions, under white rule problems of external relations were dormant. But in the 1970s the Portuguese departed from Angola and Mozambique, the Rhodesian whites were defeated by black guerrillas and South Africa came under pressures from North America and Europe as well as black Africa to give independence to Namibia. All these emergent states had – or, in the case of Namibia, seemed destined to have – governments which called themselves socialist or Marxist and were believed, or represented, by South Africa to be communist and stooges of the Soviet Union.

Pretoria's responses were unsure and inconsistent. Prime Minister John Vorster put a good face on the victory of Samora Machel's Frelimo in Mozambique, sent him a goodwill message and hoped to bring Mozambique into a quasi-Malawi relationship. In Angola, however, the incursion of 20,000 Cubans with evident Russian approval prompted South Africa to invade that country in the hope of destroying the nascent regime of Agostinho Neto's MPLA. The invasion failed, leaving some nagging questions about the effectiveness and training of the South African army and considerable sourness against the United States which encouraged South Africa and then left it in the lurch. In Rhodesia South Africa was forthright in its support of Ian Smith, did all it could to keep him afloat, was a clear loser when he sank, and then hampered Robert Mugabe's first years in office by withdrawing loaned locomotives which were essential to keep Zimbabwe's traffic and economy moving. In Namibia, where Sam

Nujoma's Swapo seemed to Pretoria most militantly anti-South African and communist-inclined, the successive governments of Vorster and Botha tried to promote an anti-Swapo regime which would be amenable to South African wishes (the Democratic Turnhalle Alliance led by Dirk Mudge, a variation on the Malawi theme) while at the same time negotiating with the five-power Contact Group (United States, Canada, Britain, France, West Germany) which was trying to arrange conditions for elections as a prelude to independence.

The entire area covered by these territories is dominated by South African power and by the uncertainties in South Africa itself about how to use that power. The power is not in question. The abortive invasion of Angola in 1975 has been repeated to greater effect and a portion of the country brought effectively under South African control. In Mozambique armed opposition to the Machel government has (unavowed) South African support in attacks on its road and rail routes, harbour installations, oil pipelines and hydro-electric works. In Zimbabwe's capital Harare premises used by the ANC have been attacked from the air and small South African units operate across the South African–Zimbabwean border, allegedly without the knowledge of their superiors. In Lesotho a cabinet minister has been assassinated by a guerrilla band coming from South Africa and late in 1982 a South African armed invasion killed about forty people. In the same vein mercenaries employed to overthrow President Albert René in the Seychelles were able to organize their abortive expedition in South Africa and use South African weapons and materials.

Even Zambia, which has no frontier with South Africa, feels Pretoria breathing down its neck. Zambia became an independent state in 1964 with high hopes deriving from its natural wealth and the character of its leader, Kenneth Kaunda. The main source of this wealth was copper but Zambia has also a well watered agriculture and was exporting food as well as copper. In the 1960s the economic product grew by about 6 per cent a year but in 1970 the price of copper, on which Zambia remained over dependent, fell disastrously and production at many mines became uneconomic. As in so many African countries the production of food was increasing less fast than the population and food began to be imported. In 1973 the white government of Rhodesia closed its border with Zambia, forcing it to route its copper by the Tanzam railway to Dar-es-Salaam instead of southward to South Africa. Zambia's participation in sanctions against Rhodesia after the illegal declaration of independence from Britain forced Zambia's balance of payments further into the red.

(The potentially rich countries of Zambia, together with Zaire and Zimbabwe to north and south of it, are all landlocked except for Zaire's outlet to the sea along the Congo river. They depend for their export earnings on an inadequate railway system consisting of three main lines. The first runs from Zaire through Zambia and Zimbabwe to the South African port of East London. The second goes from Zaire to the Angolan port of Benguela and the third is the Tanzam line from Zambia through Tanzania. This last line, built by the Chinese, has been a big disappointment owing to poor maintenance along the line and congestion in the port of Dar-es-Salaam.)

Shortages of food and work, increasing crime and the hardships accepted as the price for helping refugees from Rhodesia and guerrillas operating there, combined to weaken Kaunda's position and tarnish his reputation. A presidential election in 1978 was rigged by turning it into a one-horse race (Zambia had been a one-party state since 1973) and in the same year Kaunda was obliged for the first time to seek financial aid from Britain. He was also forced to compromise over the support given to Zimbabwean guerrillas and to Swapo in order to resume passage for his exports by the South African route. Zambia's predicament illustrates the length of South Africa's disruptive reach.

IV

The whole of southern Africa up to the southern confines of Zaire and Tanzania lives in a state of permanent semi-war. East Africa is a pattern of distrustful neighbours, a number of them recently warring and likely to resume warring with one another. West Africa does not know whether Nigeria's dominance and wealth are to be more welcomed or feared. In the north the Maghreb is a conspicuous example of a geographical expression without political or economic coherence. In every quarter the record of recent decades reinforces the judgement that visions of African unity, regional or continental, were and are the purest fantasy.

And yet . . . . In the centuries before the creation of the first unified Chinese empire (221 BC) that vast area was fragmented into kingdoms whose separate identities and ambitions would have exposed to ridicule any seer peddling a vision of Chinese unity. But that is what came about and, with it, rapid technological progress (iron casting, for example, a capital-intensive operation) and a population explosion which incurred no economic disaster. Africa does not look as though it is on the eve of emulating China's distant achievement; but if necessity is the mother of invention in the politico-economic realm Africa's necessities are enough to generate many inventions, for there is little reason to suppose that any African states bar very few can prosper, or even survive, as sovereign within their present boundaries.

6   THE STRATEGIC IMPORTANCE OF AFRICA

I

In world affairs Africa has had one huge advantage over Asia: it comes lower down the list of other people's priorities. Asia has been invaded by both superpowers and has inflicted on them humiliation and demoralization. The Americans in Vietnam and the Russians in Afghanistan committed massive forces at great cost against an enemy whom they expected to discipline quickly and cheaply. That was humiliating miscalculation. Worse: Asia took a diabolical revenge. The drug addiction visited upon the Americans by their service in Vietnam has, according to less easily verifiable reports, been inflicted on the Russians too in Afghanistan.

So perhaps both superpowers might hesitate the more before engaging themselves in similar ventures, thus allowing Africa to escape from their devastating attentions.

Yet it would be foolish to put much faith in such speculations for Africa matters to non-Africans. It matters because its geographical position gives it an inescapable importance in geopolitical strategies, particularly those of the seas and oceans. It matters too because it is exceptionally rich in important minerals. It matters again – or could matter – because its peoples constitute a large potential market for foreign goods if and when they become rich enough to buy them. And finally it matters because it is black.

This last assertion may seem strange but so long as the fortunes of the world are regulated by superpowers, one of which is the United States, then there must always be a point at which the black races beyond America may – like the Jews who are beyond America – influence or constrain American policies through the existence inside the United States of a black electorate liable to be canvassed for black causes. Moreover, as hispanics in the United States advance demographically to a position of comparable influence, there may develop an alliance between African and Latin American states which an American President may not comfortably ignore. Although less well orchestrated and less well endowed than the Jewish lobby, besides being also less united, this alliance could turn aid for the Third World into a political as well as a charitable issue in American politics.

At the time of decolonization there was a view that Africa would drop out of world affairs and be glad to do so. There were African leaders who hoped for Africa's sake that Africa would side-step the frightening prospect of involvement in the conflict between the super-powers which threatened to repeat the nineteenth century grab by the European powers. This erroneous view persisted for a time because the superpowers were slow to extend their activities into Africa. Compared with Europeans both Americans and Russians were igno-rant about Africa and, largely because Africa was in any case still a secondary theatre for them, took time to repair their ignorance. But the strategic importance of Africa has proved an irresistible lure. By the 1980s both superpowers were engaged in Africa for much the same reasons as the European powers had occupied chunks of it 100 years earlier: buried treasure and fear of each other.

Geographically Africa's main strategic importance lies in its coasts, above all in the north and northeast. North Africa constitutes the southern shore of the Mediterranean which, from Hannibal's day to Rommel's, has been self-evidently an outpost of European security. The Russo-Egyptian entente of the 1950s caused uncommon alarm in the West because of the facilities won by Moscow at Alexandria; the eviction of the Russians by Sadat in 1972 was treated in the same quarter as a major victory. At least as significant as Alexandria is the Algerian harbour of Mers el-Kebir. When the Ottoman Turks held Algiers they commanded the Mediterranean; when not, not. For any power approaching the Mediterranean from the east – Turks or Russians – Algiers is an even greater prize than Alexandria simply because it lies further westward.

The recent politics of North Africa have been a complex interplay of regional and global themes, the interests of the indigenous states interacting with those of outside powers. This long coastline is held by Egypt and Morocco at either end, each of them looking outward to the Middle East or Atlantic as well as to the Mediterranean. The central sector is held by Algeria and Libya with little Tunisia in between them.

The Soviet Union has so far posed no threat to American influence in Morocco. At the other end of the Mediterranean Khrushchev's alliance with Nasser did pose such a threat and gave the Russians a valuable base in Alexandria. It did not, however, prevent the US navy from ruling the eastern Mediterranean as effectively as the western and after Nasser's death Sadat liquidated the Russian position in Egypt. Hosni Mubarak, although possibly less pro-American than Sadat, is not more pro-Russian.

The crucial central sector of this coastline is ambivalent. Algeria, more populous and more diversely endowed than Libya, is intrinsically more important, but Libya under Gaddafi has been more vociferous in external affairs. Both countries have, since independence, become left wing but idiosyncratically so. Neither has been a tool of the Soviet Union, Algeria successfully maintaining a left-of-centre non-aligned stance and Libya too unpredictable to make a reliable dependant and too rich – so long as oil flows and sells – to need to be one.

Algeria became independent from France, of which it had been a metropolitan department since 1848, in 1962. It had to fight for its independence and was radicalized by the fight and by the departure at the end of it of much of the settled French community. It emerged therefore as a socialist left-wing state with the expectation on all sides that it would be a friend of, and befriended by, the Soviet Union. But for Algeria's successive leaders – Ahmed Ben Bella, Houari Boumedienne, Benjedid Chadli – friendship meant no more than that and Moscow has found in Algeria no obedient servants. Relations with France were soon on the cordial or at least correct side, particularly after the French evacuation of Mers el-Kebir in 1968 (the peace treaty of 1962 having given France fifteen years to get out); and when Algeria played host in 1969 to a pan-African cultural congress the foreign guests included French as well as Russian eminences. Algerians are familiar with the road to Paris, speak French and are well aware of the economic advantages of Franco-Algerian ties.

Algeria's main external concern is with Morocco, with which it went briefly to war in 1963 over a border dispute. This hostility is territorial and economic, tinged with memories of battles long ago and with ideology. King Hassan's traditional Moroccan autocracy is the antithesis of socialist Algeria and this contrast is sharpened by rival claims to mineral riches. These emotional and material antagonisms have led Algeria to back the claim of the Polisario to constitute a new state in the western Sahara, largely at Morocco's expense (see below).

Libya likewise has a special local concern which conditions its external policies. This is suspicion of Egypt. Nasser had a plan to acquire Libya or part of it; Sadat, who succeeded Nasser only a year after Gaddafi's coup in 1969, was by nature hostile to Gaddafi's messianic socialism. Gaddafi expelled the Americans from the military base which King Idris had allowed them to establish; loudly and lavishly espoused militant subversive movements from Palestine to Namibia; turned Libya into the largest *place d'armes* of Russian make outside Europe; and alarmed half Africa by intervening in the civil wars in Chad and giving rhetorical support to the notion that he was aspiring to create a new Muslim empire in Africa stretching from Sudan to the Atlantic and southward to Zaire and Gabon.

Gaddafi never had the resources for any such adventure. The population of Libya is around 3 million. Money he had from oil and he dispensed it freely at home and abroad. But Libya's economy rests solely on oil, so that it is peculiarly vulnerable to the vagaries of a single market. The mid-1970s gave oil-producers a bonanza and Libyan output, almost wholly exported, rose above 2 million barrels a day. By the 1980s this good fortune was annulled. The price explosion ceased and was reversed; the market for oil flagged as consumers reduced their demands; most of the members of OPEC resolved to cut their output and their prices; Libyan production fell as low as 600,000 barrels a day. Gaddafi found himself short of cash. The euphoric expectations of the Libyan people were checked as meat and other imported foods disappeared from the supermarket. The 1980–85 Plan was jeopardized; development projects came to a halt as foreign contractors did not get paid and, once halted, began to crumble.

Gaddafi blamed these misfortunes on the Americans. A coup against him a few months after the inauguration of Ronald Reagan was ascribed by Gaddafi (and others) to American instigation, abetted by Sadat and Nimeiri. Later in the same year (August 1981) two Libyan jets were attacked and destroyed by American missiles over the Gulf of Sirte in the Mediterranean. The pressures on Gaddafi, real and imagined, were relaxed by the assassination of Sadat in October but in November he suddenly withdrew his forces from Chad, temporarily leaving his friend Goukouni Oueddei in the lurch in spite of having scored notable successes against the rival Hissen Habre only a few weeks earlier. As his economic troubles increased he blamed the Americans, this time in conspiracy with the Saudis, for accentuating his cash problem by flooding a glutted market with Saudi oil and so making Libyan oil unsellable.

Gaddafi has always proclaimed himself non-aligned but that is no guarantee that he will remain so. To the Reagan administration Libya, and Gaddafi personally, were a serious threat to world peace because of indiscriminate support for militant movements of various kinds and for meddling in Chad.

Seen from Washington Gaddafi was a willing or unwilling tool of Moscow and therefore important. But Moscow itself was ambivalent about Gaddafi whose socialist ideas were remote from Soviet communism. Moscow supplied Gaddafi lavishly with arms for cash but became unhelpful when Libya's finances faltered. By 1981 Gaddafi was behind with the payment of interest on loans from the Soviet Union and anxious to negotiate a revised deal. But, visiting Moscow, he got a cool reception and no sign that Moscow was interested in anything except cash. Either the Russians rated his value to them lower than he would like, or they feared an open American onslaught in which they had no intention of becoming involved. A hastily arranged trip to China towards the end of 1982 betokened Gaddafi's isolation in world affairs.

One of Gaddafi's many irons in international fires was his support for the Polisario, which also had Algerian backing but was opposed by Morocco with American and other extra-African concurrence.

Shortly before his death in 1975 General Franco decided to abandon Spain's last colony on the African mainland – Rio de Oro – and hand it jointly to Morocco and Mauritania. (Spain retains now only Ceuta, Melilla and the Canary Islands.) Franco hoped that Rio de Oro would become a rather feeble state dependent on Spain, but Morocco and Mauritania wanted to partition it – Morocco in order to gain possession of the valuable phosphate deposits discovered in 1945 at Bou Craa and Mauritania in order to prevent the creation of an over-mighty Greater Morocco. Morocco, willing to compromise its claim to the whole territory in order to get part, made common cause with Mauritania against Spain and to these pressures Spain gave way, whereafter Morocco and Mauritania divided the territory two-thirds to Morocco and the rest to Mauritania.

There was, however, another party and it got the backing of Algeria and Libya. The Polisario – Political Front for the Liberation of Saguiet el-Hamra and Rio de Oro – maintained that the former Spanish territory should remain intact (following the general OAU rule in the matter of colonial boundaries) and constitute a new state called the Sahrawi Arab Democratic Republic. This state was proclaimed in 1976 in the Libyan capital and by 1978 its forces of about 10,000 men succeeded in knocking out Mauritania. But Morocco had more at stake and more stamina. King Hassan committed an army of 40,000 men. This he could ill afford but he was an astute politician who knew how to twist the American arm. After the affair of the Teheran hostages Washington set about creating a Rapid Deployment

Force capable of being despatched to the Middle East at short notice. One of its prerequisites was staging points in Morocco. So the Americans – together with the Saudis who had their own reasons for supporting Hassan as a prop of the moderate camp in the Arab world – provided arms and money; and with the money the king brought more arms from the willing French. The United States became therefore an accessory in a war to secure for Morocco the rich Bou Craa region of the western Sahara, a war at least irrelevant to American interests in north Africa and the Mediterranean and harmful to those interests in so far as it blocked relations with the intrinsically more important Algeria. Unlike France, which was more successful in nurturing its relations with Algeria, the Americans risked becoming identified with a relatively small and weak country seemingly becoming odd man out in the Maghreb.

II

For thousands of years northeast Africa and south Arabia have been linked. Their populations mingled long before the beginning of the Muslim era or even the Christian era, and the trade in incense and other valuables by sea and land established communications which can be seen as the precursors of oil's modern tanker and pipeline routes. When Freya Stark first travelled in southern Arabia between the two world wars she met tribesmen who knew Somalia and Eritrea and townspeople who had lived in Calcutta, Java and Singapore.

The strategic concept of the modern Middle East embraces all those lands which produce oil, control its passage or abut upon its maritime communications. This conglomerate area includes therefore not only Egypt but all parts of Africa in contact with the Arabian peninsula and Indian Ocean: Sudan, Eritrea, Ethiopia, Djibouti, Somalia, Kenya. With modern technology and superpower intervention this zone keeps getting bigger. Suez, once a solitary African strong point in Asian affairs, is now one of many such, including Massawa, Berbera, Mogadishu, Mombasa.

The western shores of the Red Sea are held by Egypt, Sudan and whichever of the Eritreans or Ethiopians have the better of the others. At the Bab el Mandeb at the Red Sea's southern end Djibouti, independent since 1977, looks across the narrows to South Yemen where, in 1971, the British abandoned the strategic base at Aden to a new left-wing state. Further to the south Somalia offers naval, air and communication centres which have been used by Russians and Americans in turn, while south again the Americans are establishing their power in Kenya.

These countries constitute a front in the superpower conflict but a front of a novel kind. The superpowers do not confront one another across battle lines but compete for positions along it. The front itself is therefore rarely static and is at the mercy of domestic permutations in each state of the region. The superpowers study internal movements with an eye to manipulating them for their own purposes. This has happened in Egypt, Ethiopia and Somalia. The superpower contest has had smaller impact in Sudan and Kenya because one of the players, the Soviet Union, has had a poor hand in these countries and has played it badly. Russian support for communists against Nimeiri and for Oginga Odinga against Kenyatta was in both cases a grave misjudgement. So far neither superpower has been remotely in sight of securing control along the whole front. If either of them were to do so the macro-strategic picture of the world would look entirely different, although curiously the rest of Africa would be less obviously affected than Europe and Asia.

The revolution of 1952 which put an end to the monarchy in Egypt was followed within a few years by the Anglo-French invasion of Egypt in collusion with Israel. These two events, coupled with American unwillingness to give the new Egypt substantial financial aid (for the Aswan dam in particular), turned Nasser's attention to the Soviet Union for the arms which he needed against Israel and for the funds which he needed for his economic projects. Moscow was thereby presented with an opening which it had never had before. The consequences for the Middle East do not belong to this book. In Egypt they were ephemeral. The Russo-Egyptian alliance was a bizarre partnership between two states which had neither interests nor culture in common, but it was sustained for a few years by the congruent personalities of two singular statesmen, Khrushchev and Nasser, two plain-dealers who shared the fashionable delusion that natural difficulties can be brushed out of the way by 'summit' diplomacy (that is to say, by personal intercourse between semi-informed politicians). Khrushchev's demotion in 1964 and Nasser's death in 1970 dissolved the alliance and Sadat's spectacular eviction of 20,000 Russians from Egypt at a week's notice in 1972 was a recognition of its incompatibility.

Egypt, so long as it has tolerably good relations with at least one rich Arab country, is able to pursue foreign policies reasonably independent of the superpowers (an advantage which Sadat sacrificed when he signed the Camp David agreement with Israel and the United States). Nasser ignored ideological differences in the interest of good relations with Saudi Arabia, and Hosni Mubarak has been moving Egypt back to the Arab world in order to secure the financial underpinning needed to sustain relative independence. The spread of radical regimes in the Arab world, leaving Egypt ideologically stranded, could alter this position but Egypt – like Algeria and Libya – normally has an alternative to attachment to a superpower. With a bit of help and good neighbour relations it can stand on its own feet.

Sudan is in a similar position, anxious to remain at arm's length from the superpowers but dependent on Saudi or other Arab subsidies for the means to do so. Like Egypt, Sudan is a necessitous country which has the option of pursuing in the Arab world an alternative to the superpowers as a source of economic and military aid.

Sudan has been under military rule for most of its independent existence. Independent in 1956, its first civilian regime lasted only until 1958 when it was removed by a military coup led by General Ibrahim Abboud. This coup was widely tolerated because the civilian government had failed in both its major tasks: holding a fair balance between Sudan's religious communities, and pacifying the rebellious south whether by force or conciliation. General Abboud did no better in the south and in spite of an adventitious boom in cotton exports he increasingly alienated the professional classes and the young. The civilians ruled again from 1964 to 1969 when a fresh coup instigated by younger, leftish officers gave General Gaafar Nimeiri the power which he still held in 1984. Nimeiri nationalized banks, introduced land reform, declared the country to be non-aligned, gave posts to communists and boxed the political compass until Sudan seemed to be pointing itself towards the Soviet Union and towards Gaddafi (who came to power in the same year as Nimeiri). Moscow had visions of a left-wing block stretching from Tripoli in the central Mediterranean through Sudan to the Red Sea and beyond. But once more nationalism proved stronger than ideology and an attempt to shift Sudan still further to the left had the opposite effect. A coup against Nimeiri in 1970 misfired, although not before Moscow had improvidently acclaimed it; the communist leader Muhammad Mahgoub was executed; Nimeiri's position was reinforced by some nimble political footwork and by the pacification of the south which had eluded all his predecessors. By the early 1980s Sudan under Nimeiri had an ostensible but not very purposeful left-wing regime whose sympathies in world affairs were obscure rather than non-aligned and which, like Algeria rather than Libya, put discretion before ostentation.

The west coast of the Red Sea, unlike almost the whole of its east coast, is in divided ownership. The central sector of about 750 kilometres is Sudanese. To the north Egypt occupies 1,000 kilometres. To the south lie another 1,000 kilometres which belong to Eritrea or, if Eritrea belongs to Ethiopia, then to Ethiopia. And in this query lies much of the importance of Ethiopia to the rest of the world, for without Eritrea (or Djibuti, whose inhabitants are partly Somali, partly Ethiopian kin) Ethiopia does not touch the Red Sea at all. With it Ethiopia impinges directly on the Arabian peninsula and so on the Middle East, in addition to looming over the Bab el Mandeb and projecting its influence – or the influence of any power to which it grants bases – into the Indian Ocean. At the beginning of the 1970s this power was the United States; at the end it was the Soviet Union.

The ancient empire of Ethiopia has been distinguished by its escape from European imperialism (apart from seven years under Italian rule) and its imposition of imperial rule on a number of subjected peoples: Eritrean, Tigrayan, Oromo (sometimes and disparagingly called Gallas), Somali, Afar and others. The dominant Christian Amhara minority ruled over a peasant society which hovered around or below subsistence level and produced, in feudal rather than capitalist mode, for a parasitic aristocracy. A small bourgeois class which hardly knew where it belonged played an insignificant political role. The empire collapsed in 1974 on the principle that, even for a camel's back, there is one straw too much. The straws included the spread of poverty from the countryside to the capital, student unrest and finally army mutinies. After a brief Kerensky-like interlude during which the old order tried to find a way to survive the army deposed the emperor. A military committee (the Derg) quickly suppressed left-wing, bourgeois and intellectual organizations and, despite initial promises to share power with Ethiopia's other ethnic and religious groups, confirmed Christian Amhara domination under the new leadership of Colonel Haile Mariam Mengistu.

But Mengistu's rule was severely tested by Oromo risings, a Somali invasion and intensified Eritrean separatist warfare. Mengistu was forced to seek help from the Soviet Union. Moscow decided to respond and so inaugurated the most flamboyant and most impressive invasion of Africa by an outside power since the Second World War.

When Fidel Castro responded in 1975 to the call for help from Agostinho Neto in Angola, he did so largely because Neto was a friend. The Russians in Ethiopia had no such grounds. They went to Mengistu's aid in 1977 for two reasons, both of them extraneous. The first was the geographical importance of the Horn of Africa in relation to the Indian Ocean and Middle East. The second was the calculation that even so massive an operation would evoke no American counter-measure. The Russian occupation of Addis Ababa has therefore something of the character of the British occupation of Alexandria in 1881: a spectacular move, unrelated to purely African affairs and adjudged to be low risk in spite of its high ostentation.

Mengistu's Ethiopia was revolutionary in the sense that the Derg had overthrown the empire. But it was not revolutionary in much else and Moscow did not go to its aid for ideological reasons. Moscow already had an ideological ally in the Horn in President Said Barre of Somalia but the Kremlin was prepared, if reluctantly, to jettison him for geopolitical advantage. The Soviet Union would have liked to be friends with both Barre and Mengistu but when obliged to choose decided that the latter was worth more than the former.

Somalia, compounded of the former British and Italian colonies which attained independence together in 1960, was getting Russian aid even before Barre seized power in 1969. A first military aid agreement providing for the disbursement of $35 million was signed in 1963. The importance of this link became such that in 1974 President Podgorny himself visited Somalia to sign a new ten-year treaty of military assistance and – an unparalleled benefaction – cancel Somalia's accumulated debts to the Soviet Union. The Russians developed a naval base at Berbera, an air base at Hargeisa and a communications centre at Kismayu. Some 2,000 military technicians went to work in Somalia and the equipment assembled there was worth about $1 billion. The Soviet Union's well-judged support for Barre became all the more important when Moscow lost its positions in Egypt in 1972 – in which year the Minister of Defence, Marshal Grechko, visited Somalia. Two years later the Soviet Union made new treaties not only with Somalia but also with Algeria and Libya. The fall of Haile Selassie opened the possibility of yet another attachment to put against the Egyptian reverse.

The Russians did not intervene to support Mengistu until the refusal to do so would have meant his defeat by Somalis and Eritreans. Moscow's ideal of an alliance with Ethiopia which could be reconciled with its alliance with Somalia was destroyed by Mengistu's refusal to honour his promises to the non-Christian peoples of the empire and by Barre's sense of opportunity. Upheaval in Ethiopia was a chance not to be missed and under pretext of helping the Somalis within Ethiopia Barre invaded the empire and came within an ace of annexing part of it. At this point the Russians had to choose and they chose Mengistu. They drafted Cuban troops (mostly from Cuba, some from Angola) into Ethiopia and staged an extremely impressive airlift of military hardware via South Yemen – the most dramatic operation of its kind since the Anglo-American airlift to Berlin in 1948–49. They saved Mengistu.

They saved him again next year from the Eritreans who, in spite of their own dissensions, came close to winning the independence for which they had been fighting for twenty years.

Since the importance of Eritrea is its coastline, without which Ethiopia has no access to the Red Sea and much reduced value to an ally, Eritrea's history since its liberation from the Italians in 1941 has been forcible integration into Ethiopia with the concurrence of first the British, then the Americans and finally the Russians – all of them regulating their attitudes to Eritrea by reference to their relations with Ethiopia.

The British, who conquered Eritrea during the Second World War, administered it until 1952. The principal victors in that war could not agree on what should happen to Eritrea. Nor, until 1952, could the United Nations. Solutions ranging from independence to full integration with Ethiopia, with various intermediate constitutional devices, were debated; the British wished to give part of it to Sudan and the rest to Ethiopia. In 1952 a compromise was reached and Eritrea became on paper an autonomous unit in a federation with Ethiopia. The Ethiopians never respected this agreement, proceeded to annex Eritrea but at the same time exacerbated militant opposition which they have never been able to quell.

They were greatly helped by the Americans. Within a year of the federation agreement the United States undertook to provide Haile Selassie with arms in return for permission to occupy and enlarge the Kagnew communications and intelligence centre abandoned by the British. This centre, which became one of the biggest of its kind in the world, is in Eritrea, not far from the Eritrean capital Asmara. Under later agreements both American military aid to Ethiopia and the Kagnew centre were greatly expanded.

For the Americans this centre was a factor in the global war against the Soviet Union. For the Ethiopians the military hardware was for use against the Eritreans. A further element was introduced when the Israelis agreed to train special Ethiopian military units for operations in Eritrea. The Red Sea was once more the cause: Israel wanted the Eritrean coastline to be under the control of grateful Ethiopians rather than of Eritreans who, since more than half of them were Muslim, might be expected to side with the Arabs against Israel and impede traffic to the Israeli port of Eilat. The upshot of these diverse currents was that Ethiopia, like Morocco, secured the aid of the United States and its friends for a conflict which, like that in the western Sahara, affected American interests only at second remove.

Eritrean guerrilla warfare against Ethiopia began in the late 1950s and grew rapidly. But so did the Ethiopian response based on foreign aid. Enormous destruction and atrocities ensued and over a quarter of a million Eritreans were driven into exile. The Eritreans had some help from Cuba, Libya, South Yemen and Saudi Arabia but they were divided among themselves. In 1977–78 they overcame their divisions and launched successful operations against the new regime in Addis Ababa, but just as the Americans had armed Haile Selassie from the 1950s so now the Russians stepped in with even more massive aid for Mengistu. Cuba was forced to change sides and Libya and South Yemen sheered off as the new Ethiopian offensive turned the tide of Eritrean success. By 1980 Ethiopia had an army of occupation 100,000 strong in Eritrea and half a million Eritreans were refugees outside their country. Eritrean independence was a remote dream and even autonomy a doubtful goal.

Ethiopia became as a result of these operations a protectorate of the Soviet Union which dominated, if not the whole of the country, at least its central government. Whether this was wise remained to be seen. Ethiopia tends to be more than a handful for any ruler, home grown or foreign, who tries to master it.

The American position in the zone as a whole – northeast Africa and the Indian Ocean – was considerably stronger than the Russian even after the reversal of alliances in Addis Ababa. Throughout the 1960s and 1970s Saudi Arabia was a firm friend, hardly if at all threatened by the fate which overtook Haile Selassie and the Shah of Iran. The British navy ruled the waves of the Indian Ocean until 1971 and thereafter the US navy did the same. The United States had already developed in the 1960s the A 3 Polaris missile which, with a range of 4,000 kilometres, could hit the Soviet Union from vessels in the Indian Ocean, and although this missile was not deployed in that theatre its existence was an extra incentive to expand Russian naval power which, under the guidance of Admiral S. G. Gorshkov, was one of the outstanding features of Leonid Brezhnev's period of power.

Brezhnev had correctly interpreted Khrushchev's Cuban fiasco of 1962 as a failure in the naval component of Russian world power, a failure of reach which must be urgently corrected. One consequence of his resulting naval programme was the Soviet Union's ability to keep a small squadron permanently in the Indian Ocean from the early 1970s. But it had to operate from distant Vladivostok whence its vessels threaded a long and vulnerable passage through the South China Sea and the islands of Indonesia. It was a portent but not yet a match for American sea power, which was itself reinforced in the same period by the development of a new naval base on Diego Garcia. This island, which had been part of the British colony of Mauritius, was detached before Mauritius got its independence and joined to a new colony: the British Indian Ocean Territory, created in 1965 and consisting of groups of small islands between Sri Lanka and Madagascar. The inhabitants of Diego Garcia were evicted and the island leased to the United States in 1971.

On the African mainland the Americans' loss of the Kagnew centre was offset, first, by its declining importance after the launching of space satellites and, second, by the takeover by the Americans of the positions forfeited by the Russians in Somalia. In order to guard against possible future changes in Somalia the Americans also secured Kenyan consent for the development of Mombasa as a major naval base. Yet the argument which led Washington to supplement Somali with Kenyan bases – the political unpredictability of Somalia – applied equally to Kenya where the growing American presence was an element in the abortive revolt against the Moi government in 1982. In that same year too a change of government in Mauritius put a question mark over Diego Garcia which the new government claimed to be a part of Mauritius illegally abstracted. The pattern was a shifting one – the more so because it was dominated by the adventitious manoeuvres of the superpowers rather than by the more predictable and tenacious attitudes of the local states to one another.

At the beginning of the 1980s the Russian position centred on Ethiopia while Ethiopia in turn depended on the Soviet Union and was bound to remain so dependent as long as the regime's overriding need was for arms. This dependence could be lessened only through accords with Eritreans and Somalis. The Americans therefore favoured some relaxation, partly to loosen the Russian hold over Mengistu and partly in the hope of seeing the Cubans removed from the Horn. In the absence of detente in the Horn's local feuds Washington's principal footholds were perforce in Somalia, Kenya and Djibuti – an uneasy combination since the first two of these states had one of Africa's less tractable border disputes, Somalia had a government which was both left wing and weakened by its defeats in 1978, and Djibuti was a divided state whose people looked half to Ethiopia and half to Somalia. Saudi Arabia bore witness to the Middle Eastern significance of these African rivalries by trying to mediate betweeen Somalia and Kenya, by joining the Americans in subsidizing Said Barre in Somalia (which was somewhat incongruously admitted to membership of the Arab League), by joining the French in subsidizing the regime in Djibuti, by helping the mainly but not entirely Muslim Eritreans in their war against Ethiopia, and by trying to bribe South Yemen away from the Russian embrace.

The positions of both superpowers – the Russians in Ethiopia and the Americans round about – were beset with uncertainties. The fact that they accepted these hazardous involvements attested the importance which they attached to the zone. If still hesitantly, they were in the process of committing themselves to global strategies in which this part of Africa played a necessary part.

III

No other African littoral has anything like the importance of its northern and northeastern coasts. White South Africans would like to think that the naval base at Simonstown (relinquished by Britain in 1957) comes into this category but they have failed to persuade even the Americans that this is so. On the Atlantic side Walvis Bay and Conakry are not without their attractions but they are insignificant by comparison with the arc which stretches from Mers el-Kebir to Mombasa. The strategic importance of the African south is not so much naval as mineral.

The word 'strategic' must in this context be qualified. The expression 'strategic minerals' is misleading in so far as it suggests that the chief value of these minerals is for war industries or, in reverse, for maiming an enemy's war effort by denying them to him. They have very considerable commercial value and are sought after by corporations and states, communist as well as non-communist, because of their peacetime industrial uses. The Soviet Union and eastern Europe have a genuine interest in Africa's mineral resources quite apart from their role in a shooting or an economic war.

The areas which contain these minerals – mainly southern Africa but also the northwest and other parts – have therefore assumed some of the character of the Middle East in world affairs. Like oil, mineral ores exist in finite quantities. When they are concentrated in a few countries, these countries have special economic muscle but are correspondingly exposed to the often unwelcome attentions of outside powers. Their weapons are the control over levels of production and the aberrations, sometimes contrived but sometimes automatic, of prices. In 1978, for example, when rebels in the Shaba province of Zaire occupied a mine responsible for half the world's output of cobalt, the price quadrupled. On the other hand, and again like oil, African producers are dominated by their regular western trade because of the part played by mineral exports in their economies. Zambia's mines provide 40 per cent of its GNP, 55 per cent of government revenues and 90 per cent of export earnings; Zaire and Zimbabwe are similarly dependent.

It is therefore expedient for these and many other African countries to diversify their outlets. Conversely, but conveniently for Africa, eastern Europe wants more African minerals. Whereas the Soviet Union views Africa through mainly strategic spectacles, eastern Europe's interests are commercial and competitive. To eastern Europe Africa is a valuable source which has been nobbled by the capitalist west. East Germany and Poland, Bulgaria and Romania have engaged in a stream of visits, negotiated treaties of economic cooperation, set up joint commercial enterprises and – East Germany in particular – have invested substantial sums of money. Bilateral agreements have been supplemented by joint activity through Comecon, of which Mozambique became in 1978 the first African associate member.

For the Soviet Union the arguments are different. The Soviet Union has no pressing need for Africa's minerals. Their importance is strategic but the strategic weapon is at best secondary, since its effectiveness depends on persuading Africans to stop exports to Nato countries which Africans, of whatever ideological colour, have every interest in increasing. That the United States is theoretically vulnerable is certain. It is almost totally dependent on Zaire and Zambia for cobalt (although the quantities are not great and stockpiling therefore relatively simple) and heavily dependent on southern Africa as a whole for platinum ores, fluorspar, and the group comprising chrome, manganese and vanadium. Remedies for this uncomfortable dependence include the search for substitutes, stockpiling and investment in exploring for alternative sources. None of them can await the moment of crisis. On the other hand this degree of vulnerability is not matched by the practical imminence of crisis. Nato members are theoretically threatened but the likelihood of joint Russian and African action to deny them crucial supplies is one which they view without urgent alarm.

This equanimity testifies, not to the unimportance of African minerals, but to the unreality in western eyes of any planned and prolonged menace for access to them. The more real threats are regional and therefore partial. Continuing war in the western Sahara can cut into deliveries of iron ores and phosphates to foreign customers, communist or non-communist. Disorder in, for example, Niger or Gabon would imperil the trade in uranium. But the clearest example of western economic concern has been Zaire whose mineral riches the west covets to such an extent that it allows its political and humanitarian antipathies to Mobutu to be neutered.

Zaire is a very richly endowed country ruined by colossal debts and huge corruption. By 1982 the servicing of its external debts was costing nearly $1 billion a year. Its reserves had disappeared. Its export earnings had dropped by $500 million or 25 per cent in a single year. This was the work of President Joseph Mobutu who, having risen on the shoulders of his mentor Patrice Lumumba (in whose murder he was accused by rumour of helping the CIA), became president in 1965 and inaugurated a fearful tyranny.

After establishing his political control he made himself master of the Belgian capitalist legacy and induced western entrepreneurs and bankers to pile into a seemingly pacified and reinvigorated bonanza. He started madly ambitious and often useless schemes and created a system of licensed piracy for the benefit of himself, his relations and friends. In 1974 the collapse of the world price for copper undermined the economy and by 1980 Zaire's external debt amounted to $6 billion and arrears of interest exceeded $1 billion. Mobutu survived through the support of the army, the brutality of an elite corps as appalling as the Nazi SS, the continuing support of foreign institutions too heavily involved to pull out, and the corruption of a small and servile elite. This new privileged tribe flourished in the export-orientated economy which was annexed to the traditional but impoverished economy where standards of living were as depressed as, among the elite, they were extravagantly high. Zaire is a blatant example of development which, in the hands of a few and with outside help, hurts the people as a whole instead of helping them. The national income per head is less than $200 a year, the expectation of life at birth is forty and the personal safety of the citizen is as little regarded as his welfare.

The sources of Zaire's wealth and corruption are its minerals and the outside world's need for them. This wealth and need enable Zaire to borrow lavishly abroad. Attempts by the IMF to couple credits with conditions and supervision have been sabotaged by Mobutu who takes the loans, flouts the conditions and ignores the supervisors. A new IMF programme involving phased loans of nearly $1 billion beginning in 1982 was interrupted when Mobutu failed to reduce his budget deficits and forecasts of export earnings had to be drastically cut (owing to a fall in the price of copper, compounded by interruptions to the Benguela railway). But Mobutu has been able to reckon that, however atrociously he rules, he can command foreign tolerance and support.

And military help. Twice in two years revolts in Shaba province, where Zaire's wealth is concentrated, were put down by foreign arms. In 1977 Moroccan troops with American weapons were flown to Shaba in French aircraft at Saudi expense on the plea that the lives of Europeans (mainly Belgians and West Germans) were in jeopardy. Less than a year later French and Belgian paratroops were flown to the same area in American aircraft after 130 Europeans had been killed in the course of a second revolt. The purpose of these actions was to protect the flow of minerals to western countries. What these countries were prepared to do in Shaba they were presumably prepared to do in similar circumstances elsewhere in Africa. The Russians with paid Cuban assistance, the Americans with paid French, Belgian, Moroccan and Saudi assistance, laid the continent open.

IV

In thus recognizing the strategic importance of Africa the superpowers were following the example of France. Unlike Britain and the lesser European imperialists, France did not equate decolonization with retreat or accept the notion of the relative unimportance of Africa in world affairs.

As decolonization loomed France reorganized its economic association with its African colonies. The *loi cadre* of 1956 initiated a policy of political liberalization which led in time to the dissolution of the two big French federations in Africa and the independence of their constituent colonies, but in the same period these colonies formed with France an economic union which preserved their economic links with each other and with the metropolitan power. The new states obtained financial aid, tariff concessions and support for their currencies and France took the lead in associating them with the nascent EEC by insisting on the inclusion in the Treaty of Rome of provisions for giving aid to non-EEC countries. The first convention concluded under these provisions – the Convention of Yaounde of 1964 – was made with eighteen former French colonies which were granted preferential trade terms and shared the newly created EEC Development Fund. Other parts of Africa later participated in these EEC activities but France has consistently claimed and been accorded the post of chief of the relevant EEC department in recognition of its past involvement and continuing concern for large tracts of Africa.

In return France has secured the right to keep troops in Africa. In the early 1980s there were still some 10,000 French troops on the continent from the extreme west (Senegal) to the extreme east (Djibuti). The islands of Réunion and Mayotte were still French colonies, the last having been wrenched away from the Comoros before their independence in 1975. France's African policies were evolved and controlled by *éminences grises* in a special office in the presidential palace in Paris whence they had direct access to the President and operated a network of secret information in Africa. President Mitterrand, upon succeeding Giscard d'Estaing in 1981, continued to expand French horizons from former French colonies to the whole Third World through a reorganized Ministry of Co-operation and Development which dispensed aid in the expectation of increased French influence and exports. Paris was an established centre for meetings between African leaders and personalities and every President of the Fifth Republic visited Africa regularly. Besides twice helping Zaire (as already related) France intervened actively in the 1960s to save pro-French governments in Cameroon and Gabon – but refused, in similar circumstances, to save President Fulbert Youlou in Congo-Brazzaville. Less wisely, France supported the coup by Colonel Jean-Bedel Bokassa in the Central African Republic only to regret this action when the colonel turned into an emperor reminiscent of Caligula who, again with French involvement, had to be removed in 1979.

In Chad too France did not shrink from the hazards of intervention. This country, twice the size of France with a population under 5 million enjoying an average income of about $200, is a vast, empty and poverty-stricken expanse with no modern rail, road or air communications. The people, who speak a hundred different languages, are divided about equally between Muslims and Christians with the latter probably in a minority. French rule, always uneven, achieved virtually nothing in sixty years but favoured the Christians of the south against the Muslims of the north and east. At independence government was first vested in Christian hands (Francis Tombalbaye, Félix Malloum) but revolts in the north and east – originally directed against the level of taxes and anti-Muslim discrimination – precipitated civil war and the collapse of what passed for a government. French aid failed to save it. So did attempts by Tombalbaye to come to terms with the Muslims and appease the Libyans who, particularly after Gaddafi's seizure of power in 1969, began to dabble in Chadian affairs with an eye on the Aozou strip, a slice of Chad on Libya's border supposed, on meagre evidence, to contain uranium, coveted by Libya before the advent of Gaddafi and at one time annexed to Libya by Mussolini. In 1973 Gaddafi seized the strip after failing to buy it.

Tombalbaye was suspected of moving towards a centralized monarchy like his neighbour Bokassa, but he was ousted and killed. His successor Malloum did not long survive him. Goukouni Oueddei, a northern Muslim, became president in 1979 and agreed to merge Chad with Libya. This move cost him the support of his minister of defence, Hissen Habre, and led to a new civil war within the Muslim sector, Habre counting on the support of Gaddafi's Egyptian and Sudanese enemies. Habre defeated Oueddei and the Forces Armées Tchadiennes (FAT) of the surviving Christian leader Ahmed el-Kader Kamougue but Oueddei re-entered the fight with Libya.

One effect of Gaddafi's interference in Chad's affairs was to render French interference less obnoxious to other Africans. Libya took France's place as the principal bogey, suspected of planning a vast new Muslim Saharan empire reaching from the Nile to the Atlantic and menacing the entire West African bulge and even the riches of Zaire and Gabon. More a dream than a plan, this vision acquired some substance when Gaddafi, in addition to his incursions into Chad, was accused of intrigues in a number of countries: in, for example, the successful coup against President Sangoule Lamizana in Upper Volta in 1980, an unsuccessful one against President Seyni Kountche in Niger in the same year, and the assassination of President Luis Cabral of Guinea-Bissau again in the same year. He helped to rub some of the taint of imperialism off the French. He also posed a dilemma for France. Presidents Giscard and Mitterrand were both disposed to an active French role in Africa but they were contemptuous of American paranoia about Gaddafi and anxious not to appear to be acting as Washington's stooges for Gaddafi's overthrow. When therefore war between Habre and Oueddei flared up in 1983 and Habre appeared to be on the verge of defeat, Mitterrand sent French troops to save Habre even though French public opinion was on balance opposed to becoming directly involved in the war. Unlike Reagan, Mitterrand did not see the war as an occasion to destroy Gaddafi, with whom he simultaneously engaged in discussions; he resented being prodded by Reagan into doing what Reagan was not willing to do for himself through fear of offending American opinion (already alarmed by the despatch of American military and naval forces to Central America);

but he judged it expedient to act in order to maintain France's general posture as an African power and, more specifically, to reassure France's African friends who were scared of Gaddafi – for example, Niger, a crucial supplier of uranium for the French nuclear industry.

It mattered little to anybody except themselves whether Oueddei defeated Habre or vice versa. Chad, a vast wasteland, has no strategic or economic value and Libya, a country vaster and even more sparsely populated, lacks the capacity to do anybody any serious harm there. Yet the upheavals in these deserts brought two major western powers on to the scene and into ill-disguised conflict with one another and so testified to Africa's power to command world attention and even deflect the policies of great powers.

7 THE IDEOLOGICAL FACTOR

I

Throughout their first decades of independence there has been a persuasive expectation that the new states of Africa would lean ideologically to the left and, in their external preferences, towards the Soviet rather than the western block. This belief was grounded, first, in anti-colonialism which was in the nature of things anti-western but not anti-Soviet; anti-westernism embraced anti-Americanism in spite of emphatic American hostility to colonialism. It was grounded, second, in the left-wing tone of the utterances of those anti-colonial leaders who envisaged an amelioration of African societies as well as the transfer of power from alien rulers.

But for most Africans anti-colonialism was a programme rather than a concept or ideology. It was something that had to be done, and although the programme found more sympathy with the left than the right in the western world, the left–right pattern was largely irrelevant. There was nothing particularly odd about the fact that nearly all Britain's acts of decolonization were performed by Conservative governments. In spite of western fears there was no recourse to the Soviet Union by anti-colonial movements except in those few cases where, for practical and not ideological reasons, a protracted conflict forced the insurgents to look for outside aid and arms where they could get them: in most cases outside aid was not needed.

Military regimes differ little from civilian in their ideology. The military in Africa do not conform to western stereotypes of a right-wing conservative officer caste (although they move in that direction). More often than not the military in politics have been credited with, or have claimed for themselves, revolutionary or populist or egalitarian programmes, and both types of regime – military as well as civilian – have used the word Marxist to describe their inclinations, thus greatly alarming the west and misleading the Soviet Union.

In their external relations nearly all independent African states have espoused non-alignment. But non-alignment is hardly an ideology. Nor – in Africa – has it been a cover for pro-Soviet sympathies. It was originally an expression of distaste for the conflict between the two big power blocks, compounded of the fear of being caught up in that conflict and some self-righteous condemnation of it. The non-aligned movement then developed into a pragmatic instrument wherewith the poor but numerous might put pressure on the rich few – and it has been sadly ineffectual.

On the other hand ideology is an apt word to describe one enduring element in African affairs. This is black Africa's hostility to white supremacy in South Africa. South African *apartheid* gives African politics an ideological twist and a passionate content which are inherently anti-western. So far they have not worked in the Soviet Union's favour but they could do so. If and so far as Moscow calculated that it might turn anti-colonialism and African socialism to its advantage, Moscow has been proved wrong. But anti-*apartheid* gives it a second chance. The rejection and defeat of racial inequality and racist contempt are more potent in Africa than the socio-economic doctrines of Tom Paine or Karl Marx.

II

The Soviet Union has done little to draw Africa to its side. Much of what it has attempted has been ill conceived and ill executed, half-hearted and meanly meagre, or plainly conditioned by non-African considerations (notably by power struggles in the Middle East and Indian Ocean). Initially too Moscow was exceptionally ignorant about Africa.

Unlike other Europeans, Russians had not enjoyed the advantages of generations of reporting by traders, missionaries, explorers and colonial administrators. A few nineteenth century travellers in the Nile valley, a comic-opera invasion of Somaliland and Ethiopia in the 1880s and some marginal activities by the Orthodox Church were all that Tsarist Russia had to put against the stores of Western European knowledge. Russia was excluded from the scramble for Africa in the 1880s; the Tsars ruled nowhere in Africa and, since virtually none of it was independent, had no diplomats there to report about it. The

Bolshevik revolution gave a spurt to African studies but this died away after a few years under the pressure of more urgent cares. In political terms Africa was a remote sideshow and in the academic world it ranked as a minor section of what were called Oriental Studies.

The Second World War broadened the view, at least to the further shores of the Mediterranean and to the Horn where Stalin put in a bid (which failed) for a share in the conquered Italian colonies. The Soviet Union sent representatives to the first Afro-Asian Peoples Conference (Cairo, 1955) and to the first All-African Solidarity Conference (Accra, 1958), staged a conference of Asian and African writers (Tashkent, 1958), and created a Soviet Association for Friendship with Africans (1959) and the Peoples Friendship University in Moscow (1960), later renamed Lumumba University. At the same time scholarly studies were encouraged and increased. In the 1950s the Institute of Ethnography in Moscow organized a symposium on Africa and extended the African side of its research programmes in history, economics, ethnography, sociology and languages. Opportunity began to beckon and funds to flow. In 1959 the Africa Institute was founded in the course of a reorganization of the Oriental Studies Department in the Soviet Academy and was placed under the direction of the internationally known historian I. I. Potekhin, author of a number of African studies and editor of a vast work on the peoples of Africa. The Institute was expanded in 1962 with special emphasis on economic and social questions and in 1965, on Potekhin's death, it received a new director, V. G. Solodovnikov, who shifted the emphasis from the past to the present. A year later the Academy's Social Sciences Department (the Institute's parent body) created a new coordinating Council for African Studies with Solodovnikov at its head. By 1970, according to Solodovnikov, there were 350 scholars working in the Soviet Union on African subjects and they included four corresponding members of the Academy and twenty-two who had reached the rank of D.Sc. Africa became a growth industry in the academic world and this expansion was fostered not only in the Academy itself but also in new or expanded departments in Moscow and Leningrad Universities and in universities in East Germany, Czechoslovakia, Poland and Hungary. In 1976 Solodovnikov was appointed ambassador in Zambia (with, it was reported, general supervision over the whole of southern Africa and high rank in the KGB); he was succeeded at the Institute by the son of the Foreign Minister A. A. Gromyko.

But this quickening of Soviet interest in Africa had no corresponding counterpart in Africa, notwithstanding that Moscow had the anti-colonialist field to itself for a few years. The Americans, once as stridently anti-colonialist as the Russians, muted their anti-colonialism as the Cold War brought them into close alliance with Western Europe: it was, for example, impolitic to try to get France to accept the rearmament of Germany and at the same time attack the French empire. But the anti-colonial field shrank rapidly when the colonial powers, to everybody's surprise including their own, resolved to abdicate quickly and without a fight. The British, influenced by Asian rather than African concerns, led the way; the French and Belgians were only a step behind; the tardier Spanish and Portuguese were less significant. But for the fight put up by the French in Algeria and the intransigence of the semi-independent British settlers in Rhodesia the anti-colonial drum would have been an even feebler political instrument than it turned out to be, for its efficacy depended on there being war and there was very little war.

The Soviet Union was ready and willing to arm liberation movements if only because, before independence, these movements, besides having anti-western nuisance value, were the only organizations with which Moscow could deal. But in this pre-independence phase most of the liberation movements got what they wanted without recourse to arms, so that the opportunities open to Moscow receded to the further end of an already remote continent – to the major Portuguese territories, Rhodesia and Namibia. In the event the Soviet Union did little more than was necessary to sustain its reputation for anti-colonial purity and showed a striking lack of discernment. In Rhodesia it backed the wrong horse – Joshua Nkomo in preference to Robert Mugabe – and in Angola it stopped helping Agostinho Neto and the MPLA and only resumed aid just in time to recover some credit with the ultimate winners. Africans were unimpressed.

More by accident than design the principal European colonial powers cut the ground from under Moscow's feet by the rapidity of their decolonization. In the next, post-independence phase Moscow had to find new ground. It suffered under several handicaps. Not only had colonies turned into states at a time when the Soviet Union was still very poorly informed about this part of the world. The new African leaders spoke French and English, not Russian. They were acquainted with the roads to Paris and London, but were unfamiliar with the road to Moscow and with Muscovite ways. Although they might hope to find friends in Moscow, few of them in fact had any there. For the former British colonies the new Commonwealth was an easier and more welcoming association than the Soviet block; for the French the franc zone was a surer haven. All of them were pressingly alive to their need for money and other kinds of aid which were best obtainable from the modern Croesus in the United States; and although American aid to the Third World has proved to be woefully mean, Russian aid has been even more niggardly.

But Africa's new leaders were not merely anti-colonial. Many of them described themselves as socialists. The Soviet Union had therefore a chance to build a position on what may broadly be called the left-wing ground in Africa. The outstanding fact is that they failed to do this. To Africans the Soviet Union appears a cynical great power, not a warm socialist friend.

In what was left of the Stalinist era rigid orthodoxy failed to find in Africa parties or men who measured up to requirements. Whatever they might call themselves they seemed to Moscow to be bourgeois lackeys of capitalism, forerunners perhaps of the revolution but not the genuine article and therefore not worthy of support and not worth supporting. In this area the Soviet Union cut the ground from under its own feet by looking for the impossibly limited credentials which in Europe had been gained by years of service in the Comintern but which no African – certainly no African with influence – possessed. Africa was not Europe but Stalinists approached it as though it were.

The death of Stalin in 1953 loosened the ideological logjam. Superficially this meant that the ideological line could be adjusted so as to accommodate instead of rejecting suitably left-wing African parties and states. More fundamentally it meant that policy could increasingly be dictated by practical considerations instead of pure ideological criteria so that even right-wing parties and states might be made use of by Moscow.

On the practical side this progression was marked, first, by Moscow's alliance with Sekou Toure of Guinea a few years after Stalin's death (Sekou Toure was a left-wing leader but no communist) and second, and within a remarkably short span of time, by the delivery of arms to the impeccably right-wing regime of General Gowon in Nigeria. Pragmatism prevailed over ideological sympathy even more blatantly in Egypt, where Nasser received arms even while he was holding Egyptian communists in prison, and later in Ethiopia, where Moscow intervened in force to save Mengistu after he had suppressed the left-wing movements which had made common cause with him against Haile Selassie's empire. Theoretical or doctrinal backing for this flexibility was provided under the impact of practical diplomatic necessity and broadening academic knowledge. But the dividends from this flexibility were meagre and Africa has remained a hard row to hoe for Moscow.

Stalin's death released a ferment of debate on many questions, conducted in public, in periodicals and newspapers, as well as behind closed doors. One topic was the nature of African socialism and the political direction of an independent Africa. Many Russian writers and scholars did not like the notion propounded by African intellectuals that there was something called African socialism which was different from other kinds of socialism. Ultimately, they held, there was only one true socialism, Marxist and scientific. Nevertheless it became respectable in the Soviet Union and even fashionable to point out that there might be a number of different ways towards socialism, and that Marxism might not have all the answers and or be applicable in all circumstances. So the central theoretical question shifted. Instead of asking whether a party was orthodox or heterodox, the question was whether that party was moving in the right direction. This new approach was elaborated in the first place in order to help the Soviet Union repair its relations with Tito's Yugoslavia, but the resulting latitude was also crucial for relations with the new African leaders. None of these was an orthodox communist, but under the new dispensation some might be friends and allies all the same. The object of ideological reassessment was political gain but whereas the Yugoslav leaders were as much attuned to ideological debate as Soviet leaders, African leaders were not.

The prevailing Soviet view from the late 1950s held that true Marxist and scientific socialists were rare in Africa: there were nationalist socialists, fake socialists and renegade socialists. Examples of the last two categories were Leopold Senghor whose socialist talk was the merest figment and Félix Houphouet-Boigny who had succumbed to the temptations of capitalism. Both were proceeding in the wrong direction on the wrong road. Nationalist socialists, on the other hand, could be on the right road. The signs of grace by which they could be spotted included state control of industry, banking and foreign trade and the communal ownership of land (whose African origins Soviet scholars found in a primitive socialism discernible in the tribal backwoods but viewed on the whole with disdain). These nationalist socialists belonged to a section of the bourgeoisie which was progressive and revolutionary and had chosen the path of 'noncapitalism' – a favourite phrase with Khrushchev. They had to be distinguished from other sections of the bourgeoisie which had been seduced by the departing imperialists or had fallen for the fleshpots of capitalism. In the opinion of some Soviet writers, although by no means all, this non-capitalist path could lead a state to true socialism, bypassing or skipping the capitalist phase which classical doctrine regarded as a necessary stage on the way. The nationalist or progressive bourgeoisie comprised the intelligentsia and also sections of the officer class, a surprising extension which was to come in handy when civilian regimes were replaced by the military in many parts of Africa.

The new doctrines may or may not have been an opportunist response to the facts of African politics: they were certainly opportune for, as Soviet writers freely admitted, a politically effective African proletariat did not exist. Revised practice was less than just to African communist parties which were treated as non-existent when in fact there were about a dozen of them. But some, for example the principal Senegalese Communist Party, became pro-Chinese, while others were too feeble to be worthwhile and merely got in the way of Russian dealings with governments. So the category of 'revolutionary democrats' was introduced to describe non-communists worthy of communist support, and the conference of eighty-one Communist and Workers' Parties held in Moscow at the end of 1960 endorsed the policy of befriending 'national democracies'. These were described as coalitions of progressive or non-capitalist forces and the practical effect of this definition was to widen the circle of Moscow's potential friends. Without it Moscow's diplomacy had nothing to work on, a situation which was intolerable to a restless activist like Khrushchev, a non-intellectual old man in a hurry who was ready to welcome into his embrace practically anybody who was not an out-and-out capitalist devil.

The new line was an attempt, more or less deliberate, to capture middle ground. It offended conservatives in Moscow who jibbed at sacrificing dogma and hardline communist parties but was pursued impetuously by Khrushchev who showered honours on, for example, Nasser and Ben Bella – both were accorded the dignity of Hero of the Soviet Union, an unprecedented accolade for a foreign non-communist – and invited the three West African leaders, Sekou Toure, Kwame Nkrumah and Modibo Keita, to attend the 22nd Congress of the CPSU and address it. All three were to get Lenin Prizes before Khrushchev's fall. But none of them long survived Khrushchev.

III

The post-Stalin analysis, combined with Khrushchev's personal character and with historical accidents, led the Soviet Union into optimistically close relations with these three leaders who, in Africa, came nearest to the Marxist end of the socialist spectrum. Moscow's rosy view of their three countries even caused it to discern a mass element in their ruling parties, the Parti Démocrate Guinéen, the Convention Peoples Party and the Union Soudanaise, and for a few years a pro-Soviet block in West Africa seemed to be in the making. But by the mid-1960s there was nothing left of it.

Although Ghana preceded Guinea to independence, it was to Guinea that the Soviet Union was first attracted. Pitchforked into independence in 1958 upon refusing to join de Gaulle's *communauté*, Guinea was born naked by Caesarian section. The physical and psychological traumas were severe: the stock illustration tells how the departing French took even the electric bulbs away with them. So Sekou Toure was a hero in desperate straits. He was also a hero with a communist background, although one that was thin and had worn off. He had been one of the founders at Bamako in October 1946 of the Rassemblement Démocrate Africain whose secretary, Gabriel d'Arboussier, was close to communist thinking (although its president, Félix Houphouet-Boigny, was not). He had been evicted from the French communist trade union federation (the CGT) but had then transferred to its African counterpart, the CGTA – later UGTAN – which had a communist minority. His country, though poor and thinly populated, occupied a strategic position on the south-west corner of upper Africa, its capital and chief port nearer than any other to mid-Atlantic. So Moscow was quick to give Sekou Toure diplomatic recognition, credits (140 million roubles in 1959), trade and Czech arms. He was invited to Moscow and received eminent Soviet dignitaries in Conakry. Khrushchev promised to visit him and Brezhnev did. A Soviet Ambassador was chosen with special care: Daniel S. Solod, who had served with credit as ambassador in Damascus and Cairo and seemed peculiarly well fitted to make Conakry a centre of Soviet influence and activities in West Africa.

Mali and Ghana fell more or less fortuitously into the same case. Mali (or Soudan as it still was) was the poor relation of the short-lived union with Senegal which collapsed in 1960 under the weight of its incompatibilities. Mali turned to neighbouring Guinea and was then taken up by the Soviet Union partly because it had no other friend and partly because Modibo Keita professed the same sort of socialism as

Sekou Toure. He said that Mali would skip the capitalist phase on the road to socialism. But huge, arid and land-locked, Mali had few attractions for the Soviet Union, although Bamako airport was made available for Aeroflot. Mali was offered credits of 40 million roubles.

Ghana at independence also offered little for Moscow which showed only perfunctory interest in it: no Russian ambassador went there until 1959. Nkrumah gave every sign of being a strong Commonwealth man who was happy to have the Queen of Great Britain as head of state. He spoke openly of Ghana's need for capital which, he plainly saw, must be mainly British or American. In Soviet eyes he was a typical product of the wrong section of the bourgeoisie who had won power by his readiness to do a deal with the British and whose sympathies therefore were more than half in the wrong camp.

Yet the paths of the two countries converged. Moscow had second thoughts about Nkrumah. He had been the first to give Sekou Toure practical help (£4.5 million) in 1958, he was an ardent protagonist of non-alignment in spite of his Commonwealth bias, and he played host to the genuinely revolutionary Union Populaire du Cameroon which, after first setting up shop in Cairo, later moved its headquarters and training bases to Guinea and Ghana. On his side Nkrumah became bitterly anti-American after the murder of his friend Lumumba, dismissed the British officers whom he had kept in his army, and became increasingly keen to demonstrate his non-alignment by more cordial links with the communist world. In 1960 he was offered a Soviet credit of 160 million roubles.

But things did not go smoothly. Moscow's presumptive base in West Africa might be ideological and its approach beneficent but its interest was to weaken old established ties between new states and the West and generally make trouble for the West. These were political aims not necessarily in the African interest: Africa did not want to take either side in the Cold War but to get what it could from both. Moscow's principal instrument, apart from arms, was money. Soviet credits were granted for mutually approved capital projects, to meet the balance on trading account so far as they were not paid for by Ghanaian cocoa or Guinean bauxite, and to make contributions to the training of West Africans in the Soviet Union. Moscow sought in this way to detach these states from the western economic embrace, to secure control over their exports, to plant Soviet experts in them, and win favour by great works. But the experts turned out to be more numerous than expected or desired – 3,000 in Guinea alone at their peak. They recommended grandiose works (such as a big stadium and theatre in Conakry) and the collectivization of agriculture which was not popular in West Africa and led in Guinea to unrest which the government had to suppress. Too many of the experts were ignorant of local conditions with which the departed French and British had been familiar, and they were often discourteous – an unfortunate and not exclusively Soviet trait. Initial feasibility studies proved inadequate; vastly more Russian goods arrived than were required; quality was often poor and delivery late; bills and resentment piled up.

There was dissatisfaction on the Soviet side too. When, for example, Ghana was asked to submit a list of projects to be underwritten by Soviet credits, it put forward more than 500. Whittling them down to a manageable ten was a laborious and exasperating business for the experts. There was also the price to be paid for the presumed political dividends. In 1960 the Soviet Union paid over $20 million for Ghanaian cocoa and by 1970 it was paying more than twice that sum. This commerce was more clearly beneficial to Ghana than to the Soviet Union which paid rather more than the average world price over this period as a whole. Ghana reaped a dual advantage: the Soviet Union was an assured and steady purchaser, and when world prices fell Russian purchases stayed the fall by reducing the supply to other markets and so raised the price again. Ghana used the Soviet Union as an additional market wherewith to keep prices in traditional markets more buoyant than they would otherwise have been.

These early West African ventures ended in tears. In December 1961 Solod was abruptly told to pack his bags and leave Conakry, accused of complicity in a 'communist inspired conspiracy'. This was not by any means the first plot nosed out by Sekou Toure but earlier ones had all been blamed on the French. This so-called 'teachers' plot', supposedly an attempt to sow discord among the workers and undermine Sekou Toure's increasingly autocratic regime, was said to be a Marxist-Leninist conspiracy hatched in Moscow, Paris and Dakar. Why Solod should have risked good relations with a socialist like Sekou Toure by conspiring with a feeble opposition – or whether he in fact did – has never been clear. Perhaps Solod was the wrong man for the job after all: his American colleague described him as 'cocky' and he probably indulged in some injudicious meddling. Certainly Moscow was upset by the episode, for it sent no less a personage than Anastas Mikoyan to try to patch things up. His mission was a failure and in 1962 Sekou Toure took a first step towards a more neutral stance by accepting $70 million of American aid. During the Cuban missiles crisis he refused to allow the Soviet Union to use the airport at Conakry which it had built. Ironically the first jet aircraft to land there was French.

In Ghana Moscow's calculations came to grief with the fall of Nkrumah in 1966. The new regime of General Ankrah was publicly and abrasively hostile to Moscow and expelled all its experts (about 1,000) together with the bulk of the Soviet, Cuban and Chinese embassies and the entire East German trade mission. Relations with the Soviet Union degenerated to an abusive slanging match. Modibo Keita survived in relative isolation until he was removed by the army at the end of 1968 and put in prison where he died nine years later.

Moscow's dividends in Guinea, Ghana and Mali were meagre. Sekou Touré turned nasty, Nkrumah was turned out, Keita languished; a plan by Nkrumah to make the three countries contiguous by roping in Upper Volta also came to nothing. The brief Russian experience in Guinea illustrated Moscow's handicaps and its failure to surmount them. Sekou Touré welcomed the friendship of the Soviet Union when he was alone, afraid of invasion and desperate for arms which he could get nowhere else. But by repairing his relations with his neighbours and above all with France he could dispense with Soviet aid which had in any case proved disappointing and even dangerous. In the short term he needed and got arms; but in the longer term Guinea, which does not even feed itself, needs more than arms. Moscow failed to grasp an opportunity which could have had repercussions throughout Africa. It displayed not generosity but a narrowly misconceived self-interest. Besides the one-sided bauxite venture described in an earlier chapter it refused to help Guinea to build a fishing fleet or to hand over any of the fish caught by its own fleet in Guinean waters, in well-advertised contrast with the East Germans who released a part and the Cubans who released the whole of their local catches. Ideological affinity may have led the Soviet Union to Guinea in the first place but it did little for the Guineans thereafter or, eventually, for Moscow.

IV

In the contemporary crisis in the Congo too Moscow fumbled, misled by poor political intelligence and the false lure of the ideological factor. But within a few years a different approach in the Nigerian civil war produced more gratifying results.

In the Congo crisis the Soviet Union began by endorsing United Nations intervention. When the Belgians left the likely winner in the race for power was the man whom they themselves had picked, Patrice Lumumba, and Lumumba fitted Moscow's identikit of an African socialist of the more promising variety. But Lumumba was first ousted (in September 1960) and then murdered (in February 1961) whereupon Moscow attacked Hammerskjöld's handling of the situation and threatened to intervene separately in Orientale Province to support Lumumba's political heir, Antoine Gizenga, in revolt against Lumumba's successors in the capital. Only its three West African friends and Nasser's Egypt followed Moscow's lead. The great majority of Africans rallied to Hammerskjöld, whom they regarded as the weak states' friend. Gizenga had no adequate backing either in the Congo or outside it. His revolt wilted and was doomed when Sudan refused to allow Egyptian or Russian forces to cross its territory to succour him. Gizenga's bid for power forced Kasavubu and Tshombe into temporary alliance; its collapse enabled the former to do without the latter and when Kasavubu gave Gizenga a post in the government he was a spent force and no use to the Soviet Union. When in 1965 Mobutu – the Americans' great black hope – seized power, he closed the Soviet embassy. The Soviet Union retired hurt.

The next test came in Nigeria, the least left wing of African states south of the Sahara but arguably the most important: therefore a country where political orthodoxy could not find much room for manoeuvre but one where a modest gain would count for much.

The Soviet Union – no less than the West, if for different reasons – is biased against military regimes and in Nigeria in particular it distrusted the feudal, pro-British upper crust in the North, exemplified by General Johnson Ironsi, the first of the country's military rulers. Moscow's sympathies lay with the discontented East, while in earlier years it had reposed some hope in the Western Chief Obafemi Awolowo, if only because he called himself a socialist and had been the leader of the opposition to the Northern-dominated government formed at independence in 1960. Nevertheless Soviet criticism of the Nigerian military was quickly muted. There were good practical reasons for these second thoughts. Let down by its civilian friends in West Africa Moscow was beginning to see some virtue in military men. Soldiers did at least provide stable government – or so it was thought. They were, in Bismarck's phrase, *bündnisfähig*: people with whom one could do business and make deals without finding that next day they were no longer there. Theory too was discovering good points in the military. Officers could be emanations of popular and progressive forces, sweeping away bourgeois capitalist hangovers. Then, as Moscow followed events step by step, Ironsi was succeeded by Gowon who was not a Northerner, might even be a check on the predominance of the North, released Awolowo from prison and – so Moscow wrongly imagined – might make him Prime Minister. Next, as it became clear that the Ibo leader Odumegwu Ojukwu meant to secede, Moscow's pro-Eastern sympathies were stifled because nearly all the members of the OAU were opposed to the Biafran secession and Moscow intended nothing as inexpedient as offending them. Moscow also detected, or professed to detect, international capitalist monopolies behind Ojukwu's Biafra – a new Katanga to be fortified, milked and controlled by the West. So Moscow went the whole hog and armed Gowon's government.

The negotiations were carried out with quiet professionalism. They had been preceded by non-military economic discussions. Early in 1967 Lagos announced that it was willing to take loans from the Soviet Union and its European satellites. This was a significant move by a country which had been markedly cool towards communism and communists and which – in spite of the arrival of a Soviet ambassador in Lagos a few months after independence in 1960 – had not bothered to return the compliment until 1964. A small Soviet five-man team spent four weeks in Nigeria, studying the possibilities for a steel industry and travelling over many parts of the country. (The Soviet Union eventually in November 1968 promised credits of $140 million, mostly for this project.) When civil war broke out in July all Gowon's problems were reduced to one: getting arms. The United States and Britain refused to sell him what he wanted and he turned to the Soviet Union as a last resort. The deal was done quickly and skilfully, largely thanks to the Soviet ambassador, Alexander Romanov.

Romanov combined the virtues of old school and new school diplomacy. He was an adept negotiator with, in addition, the sensitivity and geniality which make all the difference to encounters between old worlds and new states. He did not try to exploit Nigeria's urgent needs by driving a hard bargain (Lagos in any case was ready to pay cash) and he offended no susceptibilities. He understood that Nigeria could not be made communist but might be made friendly. Within weeks of the outbreak of hostilities Soviet aircraft and Czech arms began to arrive and thereafter Moscow supported Gowon firmly and openly. The goodwill created in those critical weeks has persisted. Soviet diplomacy in Nigeria aimed at and achieved limited returns. There was never any question of turning Nigeria into a satellite or even into a left-wing state, but a more tempered association was worth pursuing and was successfully pursued.

The Nigerian civil war liberated Soviet policy in Africa from its worst ideological constraints. The ideological background could not be dumped at a stroke and much of the ideological rhetoric remained. Consequently greater freedom of action was bought at a price in consistency and clarity, as the practical pursuit of power political ends clashed with attempts to retain the tattered remnants of the old revolutionary populist image. This shift was executed in response to Nigeria's practical demands and thus further discounted the significance of ideology on the African side.

V

Two developments underlined the discrepancy between Soviet actions and Soviet rhetoric: the incursions of the Chinese and the Cubans. The Chinese, by challenging Moscow's ideological rectitude, kept the ideological issue alive. The Cubans were wafted to Africa on ideological wings but stayed there for completely different reasons.

Like Moscow's, Peking's interests in Africa were primarily extraneous to Africa. The first of these concerns was to seek international recognition for Mao's communist regime and, more specifically, votes at the United Nations which would be cast in favour of the transfer of the permanent Chinese seat in the Security Council from Taiwan to China proper.

A second concern, which arose when Sino-Soviet friendship turned into Sino-Soviet rivalry, was to make trouble for the Russians. The conflict between Peking and Moscow, unlike the alliance between them, could be furthered in Africa. The alliance broke apart for two main reasons: first, because Peking became convinced that it could get no partnership with the Soviet Union except as a very junior partner; and second, because Moscow refused to be as strongly or hazardously anti-American as Peking wanted it to be. China accused the Soviet Union of domineering over its friends and of timorousness towards their common enemy; it even went to the lengths of accusing Moscow of contemplating a reversal of alliances, betraying China in order to do a deal with the United States. The split was exceedingly bitter and gave Peking additional grounds for operating in Africa besides seeking friends and votes there. Its main instrument was to outflank the Soviet Union on the left by espousing liberation movements, the more revolutionary the better, and to impugn Moscow's left-wing credentials by preaching an uninhibited radicalism of which Soviet pragmatism was growing distrustful.

This policy was first seen not in Africa but in Iraq where, at the revolution of 1958, Peking advocated unadulterated support for the local communists, however feeble they might be, whereas Moscow was readier to back whichever anti-Hashemite forces were likely to prevail. China's revolutionary purism was then extended to Africa, partly perhaps out of ideological commitment and intellectual consistency but more evidently as a means of discrediting the Soviet Union. At first this extra anti-colonial voice was welcome to Africans, but as more liberation movements graduated to independence and government, China's emphasis on subversion became less appealing and the revolutionary strain in China's rhetoric lost much of its relevance, leaving an anti-Soviet polemic which, as early as 1963, led Nyerere to speak of a new scramble for Africa between – so he implied – the Soviet Union and China. In this view Africa is more relevant to China's world policies than is China to Africa's needs; and whereas in the 1960s the West reacted with hysterical alarm to the appearance of the Chinese in Africa, Africans themselves judged more realistically: that the Chinese are nice people from a long way away who behave more agreeably than Russians or Americans but have even less to offer.

China opened an embassy in Cairo after the Bandung conference of the non-aligned states in 1955; it recognized Sudan at independence in 1956 but gained counter-recognition only after the coup in Khartum in October 1959; it was the first to recognize the FLN as the provisional government of Algeria (1958), but the Algerians were divided about accepting Chinese aid and in 1962 China, unlike the Soviet Union, disapproved the terms of the Franco-Algerian agreement which ended the war of liberation. Further afield China was hard on Soviet heels in West Africa. It was represented at the curtain-raiser for African independence at Accra in 1957 and won Ghanaian recognition two years later; it was loud in support of Sekou Toure in 1958 and joined in offering him aid (Guinea is one of the few places in Africa with a sizeable Chinese population – Madagascar, Mauritius and South Africa are others); it offered Guinea credits of $26 million and Ghana and Mali $19.5 million each, sums much smaller than the Soviet offers but free of interest and repayable over exceptionally long periods. But these were little more than gestures. When the Cultural Revolution reduced all Chinese aid to a trickle, only about 15 per cent of Chinese credits had been taken up.

In the Congo China gave Lumumba £1 million. It opposed all UN operations in the Congo, mainly because it was still denied UN membership. After Lumumba's murder it supported Gizenga until he made his peace with Kasavubu and subsequently, but with little effect, gave aid to the revolts of Mulele and Soumaliot in 1964 by helping to train recruits in guerrilla camps. In the end Mulele and Soumaliot were no more than additions to Peking's collection of broken reeds.

In the winter of 1963–64 Zhou En-lai judged the time expedient for a personal visitation. His itinerary, which embraced ten countries, showed the seriousness of Chinese interest in Africa but produced little encouragement for him. In Cairo Nasser went out of his way to make flattering remarks about the Soviet Union. The Algerians were restrained in their thanks for services rendered. His reception in Ethiopia was chilly because of Chinese aid for Somalia – where, shortly after Zhou's visit, the pro-Chinese element in the Somali government was thrown out. In West Africa only Mali gave him a welcome which could be described as rapturous. Projected visits to Nairobi, Kampala and Dar-es-Salaam had to be cancelled because of the mutinies which occurred in all three capitals. Zhou's main gain had nothing to do with his tour. In January 1964 France recognized the communist regime in Peking and most of francophone Africa followed suit and allowed Peking to open diplomatic missions (Ivory Coast and Cameroun were the exceptions). But at least China's stake was not great. In the decade between Bandung and the Cultural Revolution China's offers of aid had risen to no more than an annual $200 million (1964) and the number of African students in China was around 300. The main thing about the Chinese in Africa was how strange it was that they should be there at all.

Between Zhou's tour and the outbreak of the Cultural Revolution the position became even dimmer. The spate of military coups in West Africa was not to China's advantage; the new rulers distrusted China. Fresh opportunities in Central Africa turned into mirages. Early in 1963 a strange figure arrived in Burundi. He was Kao Liang, a political activist and journalist, who had been thrown out of Indonesia a few years earlier. His doings in Burundi were not a tribute to Chinese sagacity, for although Burundi was a scene of troubled waters there was nothing to be got from fishing in them. The successful revolt by the Hutu of neighbouring Rwanda against their Tutsi overlords after the end of Belgian rule in 1962 had brought Tutsi survivors to Burundi where they were plotting a counter-coup with the help of their Burundi kinsmen, who were still in power. There was no ideological justification whatever for communist support for the feudal Tutsi but somebody – perhaps the enterprising Kao Liang looking for a good story for the New China News Agency – must have thought that there was some mileage to be made out of helping them. At any rate China backed the Tutsi expedition to the extent of training a number of Tutsi in China in guerrilla warfare. But the expedition was a fearful disaster. It was the signal for appalling massacres in which rivers really did run blood red. In Burundi Chinese meddling was viewed with suspicion. The government split into pro- and anti-Chinese groups. The king, who was among the latter, dismissed his pro-Chinese prime minister, and when his successor was murdered the Chinese were rumoured to have had a hand in the deed. Their diplomatic mission, which had only recently arrived, was thrown out. The whole episode was murky and pointless but since the world's press paid little attention to this darkest part of Africa China earned less odium than it deserved for its extraordinary folly and cynicism in aiding a feudal razzia which failed.

No less ill fated was a parallel venture in Congo-Brazzaville, which was one of the batch of francophone African states to recognize Mao's China in 1964. A big Chinese embassy was opened, a new focus – so it appeared – for Chinese activities and influence in Africa. The prime minister, Alphonse Massemba-Debat, was well disposed to China and went there to sign a treaty of friendship which was the prelude to an aid programme. But in 1966 a military coup removed the pro-Chinese party and China's monument in Brazzaville is a white elephant of a congress hall. While the Russians were refining their political ideas and techniques, the Chinese touch in Africa was still unsure.

During the Cultural Revolution China closed all its embassies in Africa and sent back home all the African students which it had received. Its aid dwindled from about $200 million in a year to less than $15 million. After the ferment subsided it began to pick up the threads again. The most striking of its new projects was the agreement signed in 1970 to build the Tanzam railway.

Tanzania already held a special place in China's strategy. Before the Cultural Revolution the Tanzanian vice-president, Rashid Kawawa, got a warm welcome in Peking, an interest-free loan and promises of help from technical experts whose board and lodging would be much cheaper than the Russian equivalent. By contrast Kawawa had a chilly reception in Moscow where he was refused military aid and was offered help for only a few economic projects on tough terms. In 1965 Zhou En-lai visited Dar-es-Salaam at Nyerere's invitation and Nyerere went to Peking. The head of the African department in the Chinese Foreign Office was sent to Dar-es-Salaam as ambassador and on the eve of the Cultural Revolution a quarter of all Chinese aid to

Africa was going to Tanzania ($45.5 million).

And then came the railway. The railway was not a Chinese idea but it fell into China's lap. Both Nyerere and Kaunda tried to get finance for it elsewhere but they failed and it was China which agreed to advance the estimated cost of £166 million and to do so free of interest.

There were at independence no rail links between Tanganyika and Zambia. Kaunda had already spoken of the need. He was particularly anxious to create a passage for Zambia's minerals which would not have to go through Portuguese territories and both he and Nyerere saw the railway as a means of developing neglected areas in their two countries. When Zambia became independent in October 1964 the railway was in many minds. The problem was to build it.

Earlier that year China offered to help with the building of railways inside Tanzania and in 1965 that offer was extended to the projected international Tanzam line, for which Kaunda and Nyerere were known to be seeking Western help. Kaunda, still a stranger to the Chinese, was not keen. He preferred the idea of an Anglo-Canadian consortium, but then UDI in Rhodesia made his economic and communications problems more pressing and also muddied the good view that he had hitherto taken of Britain. The studies and negotiations took time but in 1967 Kaunda went to Peking and in November a first tripartite agreement was signed. Final agreement followed in July 1970 and work began that year.

The Tanzam railway was both an engineering and a political achievement. It is a single-line track 1,200 miles long with ninety-one double-track stations. It was finished two years ahead of schedule. On completion it became the property of Tanzania and Zambia in equal shares and they were to repay the Chinese loan by 1982. 15,000 Chinese were employed in its construction; they volunteered for the job and did two-year stints. They set a good example at work and behaved themselves when off. There was some propaganda by-play but when the two African governments objected it was restricted to handing round the works of Mao – a latter-day version of the distribution of the Bible by Christian missionaries.

The Tanzam railway was much talked about as a model of what foreign aid should and could do for Africa. At first it did the Chinese a lot of good in African eyes but after a time the gilt began to wear off. It was one thing to build a railway and another to keep it spick and span and punctual. Maintenance was poor, services degenerated and the Dar-es-Salaam terminal became clogged to the point of immobility. For these shortcomings the Chinese, who had done what they had promised to do, were not responsible, but their repute suffered none the less when the railway ceased to be one of the wonders of the modern world.

Throughout the 1960s and 1970s China had no direct connections with Africa. Whereas Aeroflot was operating scheduled services between the Soviet Union and some thirty African airports, Chinese airways were flying none. Nor was there any direct shipping link between China and Africa. Chinese trade to and from Africa was mutually negligible. That the Chinese should appear in Africa at all in this period was so astonishing that ridiculously inflated notions were conceived about what they were up to, what they were capable of, and even how many they were. Their achievements were in fact miniscule, but they made some headway. On the eve of the Cultural Revolution they had secured modest diplomatic recognition, and after returning to the scene they quietly took over embassies previously occupied by the Taiwan regime – some of them in countries which they would have found it difficult to enter if the Taiwanese had not got there first. A number of their smaller projects – notably those connected with rice cultivation in, for example, Guinea, Mali and Botswana – have been useful and although the volume of their aid has been small even by Russian standards, some has deserved and earned genuine gratitude. Chinese broadcasts to Africa, which began in Arabic and were directed to Egypt at the time of the Suez war, do not equal Moscow's either in number of hours per week or in the number of languages used but they are not far behind. They are tediously concerned to blacken the Soviet Union rather than advance positive Chinese views but the network and the effort are there to prove that China thinks Africa matters.

In spite of their rhetoric the Chinese have not been agents of revolutionary change, if only because they have too often backed the wrong people or the right people too feebly: in Angola they managed to help all major liberation movements except the one that won. But China has evinced interest and has established a presence which is unlikely to be removed and which may, with patience, be profitably extended. The 1970s were for China what the 1950s were for the Soviet Union – a time to learn about and probe a distant and still largely unknown and inaccessible continent. China's day in Africa has not yet come.

VI

The Cubans on the other hand have probably passed their eccentric peak.

Their arrival in Angola in 1975 was both a phenomenon in itself and the curtain-raiser for the final act in the liberation of Africa from European rule. It led to the encampment on African soil of communist armies of, eventually, about 50,000 men; and it opened a phase in African affairs in which South Africa's *apartheid* was central – the one African issue which the Soviet Union may exploit against the Western block so long as Washington and its allies prevaricate over it.

First, the Cubans and why they went there. Angola was not the first country in Africa to which Fidel Castro sent his countrymen. He was moved to intervene in African affairs by his radicalism and by his consciousness of Cuban kinship with Africa. It always beckoned him. Cuba was too small for him, and when his attempts to duplicate his revolution in Latin America failed he turned to Africa. 'African blood,' he has said, 'flows in our veins', and when he calls Africans his brothers and sisters he is expressing something that is real to him, however romantic. He wants to help them. His innate exuberance builds up a sense of international duty which urges him to contribute wherever possible to armed struggles against imperialism, colonialism and capitalism.

In 1961, within two years of his triumph in Cuba, he sent instructors to help train guerrillas in camps in Ghana – an obvious move for a proved guerrilla leader. It was at that time a limited move. The men he sent to Ghana did not fight and were not meant to. They were providing a kind of technical aid – militant technical aid. Two years later, in 1963, a second mission of the same kind went to Algeria, but when Algeria and Morocco became involved in border fighting Castro sent Ben Bella three shiploads and one aircraftload of military equipment, including tanks which were accompanied by Cubans who knew how to maintain and operate them. These Cubans would almost certainly have gone into battle in their tanks if the fighting had not stopped just before they reached the firing line. One thing was leading to another. Castro's combat units were withdrawn by the end of the year although the training mission stayed on until the overthrow of Ben Bella in 1965.

Castro was also involved, briefly and unproductively, in the Congo maelstrom. Cuban advisers, a small fighting force of about 200 with Che Guevara in person, went to the aid of Lumumba's radical heirs but the Mobutu coup in November 1965 put an end to this venture. The training mission in Ghana was wound up the next year when Nkrumah fell and for a while the only remaining Cuban presence in Africa was a small team of advisers which crossed the Congo river from Zaire to Brazzaville at the time of the Mobutu coup.

In the decade that followed Castro persisted in his role of instructor to liberation movements and branched out into a new form of aid: establishing and training internal security forces and presidential bodyguards. This reanimation of Cuba's involvement in Africa was a consequence of the tide of independence which placed more than a dozen new presidents in the palaces of colonial governors. It was also evidence of Castro's personal dedication to Africa. He might have abandoned the continent after 1965–66 without loss of face, but he chose not to.

Brazzaville and Conakry became the centres for this second phase. The choice of Brazzaville was fortuitous: it was the place where the remnants of the Congo expedition ended up and stayed. Conakry provided a second base because of its left-wing regime, its comparative geographical accessibility to the Caribbean and its involvement with the Portuguese in Guinea-Bissau to the northwest. The anti-Portuguese movements were the motor of Cuba's African policies for the next ten years.

Guevara made contacts with these movements in 1964 and Cubans were soon helping to train guerrillas for Agostinho Neto's MPLA in Brazzaville and for the PAIGC in Guinea. At the same time Castro was drawn into defending the rulers of these two host countries. He helped to foil a coup against president Alphonse Massemba-Debat (who was then happy to see the Cuban force doubled) and accepted a request from Sekou Toure to organize an internal security force and a presidential guard for him. These Cuban instructors left behind them a sensible presence of their mission in pupils who continued to sing songs and give orders in Spanish.

The overthrow of Massemba-Debat once more reduced the Cuban presence in Africa to a shadow but it never entirely disappeared and a few years later Cubans were setting up a presidential guard for President Siaka Stevens in Sierra Leone. More adventurously, if outside Africa, Castro agreed in 1973 to provide military training for the forces, including the pilots, of South Yemen and this commitment extended yet further to the east with help for the rebels of PFLOAG (Peoples Front for Liberation of Oman and the Arabian Gulf) in Oman's province of Dhofar where Cubans and South Yemenis became actively involved in the sporadic fighting that went on until the Sultan of Oman gained the upper hand in 1975 with British and Iranian help and South Yemen abandoned PFLOAG. In 1973–75 Castro also had a token force alongside the Syrians on the Golan Heights. These expeditions to the Middle East recalled that to Algeria ten years earlier when the line between training and fighting had first been overstrained. It was soon to be overstepped with a vengeance – in Angola and Ethiopia.

Angola must have engendered more liberation movements than any other country. One writer lists nearly 100 of them. However, they sorted themselves into three major groups, of which Holden Roberto's FNLA looked consistently the most effective. Roberto was distinctly anti-communist and had close ties with the pro-Western capitalist Mobutu in neighbouring Zaire. The Soviet Union had either to find another client or stay out of the game. The record suggests that there were divided counsels in Moscow. Agostinho Neto and his MPLA were suitably leftish, non-capitalist candidates for Russian aid but Moscow first backed them and then, in the year before the Lisbon coup that led to Portugal's abdication, cut its aid to a trickle. Neto turned in desperation to Sweden and Cuba (China would not help because of the Soviet connection). The Lisbon coup, which seems to have taken Moscow by surprise, caused it to reinstate its aid to the MPLA but meanwhile Roberto's FNLA had been substantially re-inforced and was ready to attack Neto and the MPLA.

Roberto's aid came from various places. During a visit to Peking at the end of 1973 he received lavish promises from China, which had been helping the third main group, Unita led by Jonas Savimbi, in a small way. After the Lisbon coup a strong team of Chinese instructors arrived at Roberto's headquarters in Zaire, to be followed later in the year by more instructors and 450 tons of weapons. Roberto also got aid from Libya and Romania as well as Zaire. Washington, which stuck to the Portuguese until the last moment, gave Roberto only token aid until early in 1975 when it switched to him the bulk of what it had been giving to the Portuguese. Thus diversely fortified Roberto took the offensive and nearly wiped out his main rivals. Moscow promptly rushed supplies to Neto by air via Conakry and Brazzaville and also by sea, thereby tilting the balance and in effect saving Neto. At this point the Chinese mission left the FNLA headquarters rather than try to match Moscow's involvement with Neto, and Romania gave up too as soon as it saw Moscow's clients fighting back and winning.

But the MPLA's successes settled nothing. The Americans were determined to thwart the advent of a left-wing government in Angola beholden to the Soviet Union. They were, however, ill placed to prevent it, not only because they had overrated Portugal's will and capacity to hang on but also because, in the immediate aftermath of their defeat in Vietnam, neither the Congress nor the public was willing to finance a military adventure in Africa for which they had not been prepared. Dr Kissinger was therefore forced into clandestine manoeuvres, using the CIA (on what that organization regarded as a shoestring) and a South African government no less determined than the Americans to prevent a left-wing lodgment on its borders. So on 14 October, four weeks before the date fixed for Angolan independence, South Africa invaded that country. On 11 November the MPLA declared itself the provisional government, other Africans rushed to recognize it and to denounce the South African invasion and its American sponsors, and Nigeria gave Neto $20 million. Yet Neto's position was precarious and he was saved, this time, by Castro.

Castro had been helping the MPLA in a mild way for many years. Neto was a personal friend and Portuguese rule in Africa was his principal bugbear. When the Soviet Union turned cool on him Neto addressed himself to Castro among others. The resumption of Soviet aid towards the end of 1974 took the urgency out of his appeal, but Cuban aid was stepped up during 1975; some 230 advisers arrived in April and were distributed over four MPLA camps; further contingents arrived in September and there were 1,000–1,500 Cubans in Angola when the South African invasion in October changed the whole course of events. Neto appealed to Castro for combat troops on 5 November. The first units arrived by air two days later.

The South African invasion was a threat to Castro's men as well as to Neto. There is no evidence that Castro anticipated it or that he intended to become engaged in war against the vastly more powerful South African Republic. But when faced with the decision whether to pull his men out or reinforce them by building up an army on African soil he did not hesitate. He determined to protect his stake in Angola by enlarging it. He hated South Africa for its *apartheid* and its capitalism. He may have sensed the hidden hand of his enemies in Washington behind Pretoria's forward policy. His natural ebullience must have reinforced his inclination to have a go. But he cannot have failed to see a big gap between the wish and the deed. Cuba and Angola lie 6,000 miles apart; and not only was the battlefield a long way away, the battles must be almost impossibly expensive for a small country which was still grappling with a major economic crisis. Soviet encouragement and finance were therefore crucial, and he had them.

The first contingent of what was to become an army of 20,000–30,000 flew to Angola on 7 November – eighty-two men in civilian disguise. This was four days before independence day and two weeks after the South African invasion. The first sea-borne reinforcements arrived on 27 November and this first ocean crossing was followed by forty-one more during the six months of active hostilities that ensued.

At one point no fewer than fifteen ships were at sea on an eastward course at the same time, a procession of men and material larger than anything of the kind since the Americans had sailed to North Africa and Europe in 1942–44 to do away with Hitler. The sea-borne effort was supplemented by an airlift. The Atlantic stretch was a testing one for Cuba's antiquated Britannias which made the crossing by landing at Barbados and then flying on to Guinea-Bissau and Brazzaville. The Barbados staging point was cut out when, under American pressure, refuelling was refused but an alternative was improvised in the Cape Verde islands until newer and better aircraft were made available, presumably by the Soviet Union.

The Cuban expedition to Angola was a gamble that came off. Its failure might have been the end of Cuban intervention in Africa, even perhaps of Castro's rule in Cuba itself. But Castro's decisiveness, translated into logistical practicability by the Soviet Union, scored a victory for Neto over the South Africans and their indecisive and covert American allies. What, however, Cuban intervention did not achieve was final victory for Neto over his internal rivals, and so Cuban troops had to stay. This can hardly have been Castro's intention. Although his expeditionary force included large numbers of volunteers, it amounted also to a fair proportion of the entire Cuban army (about 160,000 strong at this date) and Castro almost certainly hoped and expected to have the bulk of them home within months. He is reported to have taken the decision to withdraw as early as March 1976 but Neto's imperfect control over Angola has kept them there to this day.

The Cubans in Angola are the outward and visible sign of the creeping extension of the superpower conflict to the African continent and the waters round it. They are also something more. Because these surrogates of Soviet power are lodged in southern Africa, and because southern Africa is simultaneously the scene of racial war, there exists a fearful possibility. These two conflicts, the one global and the other African, may coalesce and if this occurs, then ideological emotions will be profoundly stirred and black Africa may for the first time swing right away from any friend of white supremacists and into alliance with any power which declares itself, and shows itself, to be a convinced and practical enemy of *apartheid*.

VII

Ideology is ill at ease in international affairs. Political philosophers, concerned above all with liberty and equality, have directed their critiques at the powers of the sovereign state. It needs an enormity like the slave trade to make ideology effective in the international field and propel governments into interfering in the affairs of other governments. To Africans – and not only to Africans – the theory and the practices of *apartheid* are an enormity, an international issue (because a moral one) which transcends their several national imbroglios and entitles them to ask outside powers to declare where they stand and to act.

For their part the outside powers – or at least the Western powers – desperately hope that the South African whites will ease the Western dilemma by reforming their own society with the minimum of outside pressure. Yet this hope is tenuous, for reform means power-sharing and power-sharing is still overwhelmingly rejected by a white minority which regards intransigence as both preferable and practicable. Black pressures, domestic and external, are less than compelling; and the Americans, British and other whites are most reluctant to apply any pressure that adds up to more than expressions of unease and distaste. The question is how far and how fast this balance may shift so as to cause the dominant South African whites to re-think and reverse their insistence on unqualified white power. The urgency comes from two interrelated considerations: first, delay increasingly alienates what may be the last generation prepared to listen to white proposals and, second, South Africa's unresolved racial problems may turn southern Africa's chronic regional warfare into superpower conflict.

This spectre is new. It dates from the transformation of the map of this area in the second half of the 1970s. After the departure of the Portuguese and the triumphs of Samora Machel and Agostinho Neto in Mozambique and Angola both countries concluded treaties of friendship with the Soviet Union (1977 and 1976 respectively). Shortly afterwards the whites in Rhodesia were forced to acknowledge defeat and give way to Robert Mugabe who won power by fighting for it and established the new black state of Zimbabwe in place of the short-lived hybrid called Rhodesia-Zimbabwe (in which the whites had hoped to retain, through the complaisant Bishop Muzorewa, a controlling voice). Mugabe, Machel and Neto were all socialists of a kind. So too is Sam Nujoma, the leader of Swapo which is heading for control in Namibia unless stopped by South African arms. The presence of the Cubans in Angola deepens the left-wing colour of this encirclement of South Africa.

Throughout the area the initiative lies with South Africa provided it can make up its collective mind what it wants to do with the greatly superior military and economic forces at its command. With half its mind South Africa seeks pragmatically to make the best of a bad situation. For two decades it has had correct diplomatic and active economic relations with Malawi on the basis that Malawi is economically at South Africa's mercy; and Vorster seemed at first ready to establish a similar relationship with Samora Machel in Mozambique. But in Angola the Cuban presence caused Pretoria to choose more militant tactics, invading the country before and after independence, occupying part of it, and giving Jonas Savimbi's Unita enough military support to keep him pugnaciously in the field against the government in Luanda.

Yet both the velvet glove and the iron fist have been used with circumspection. In Mozambique South Africa has combined the appearance of propriety with support for anti-Machel guerrillas (the MNR) who, established in 1976 with white Rhodesian help but initially not very effective, were resuscitated around 1980 by South Africa and equipped to conduct operations in different parts of the country under South African direction. In Angola, by contrast, South Africa has been careful not to push its aggressive policy to the point where the Angolan government may feel obliged to launch Cuban troops against South Africans. And policy in Angola has become increasingly a function of policy in Namibia where South African ambivalence is most in evidence.

After long and ineffectual battles over the status of this mandated territory its situation was transformed by the political and military events of the late 1970s which compelled South Africa to contemplate independence. But South Africa is not compelled to concede independence. It may prefer to hold the territory by force of arms and it has the capacity to do so. As an alternative Pretoria has toyed with attempts to create an anti-Swapo multiracial coalition – the Democratic Turnhalle Alliance (DTA) – which would have an adequately plausible claim to rule and be adequately friendly and submissive to South Africa.

Three things have stiffened South African attitudes from 1980 onwards. The first is the failure of the DTA to emerge as a credible vote-getting alternative to Swapo. This failure removed Pretoria's compromise option between, on the one hand, maintaining direct rule and, on the other, ceding independence to a left-wing movement which it regards as communist and a tool of Moscow. Second, the election of Ronald Reagan to the American presidency meant the prevailing in Washington of anti-communism over anti-*apartheid*. The new administration evolved a casuistic distinction between totalitarian and authoritarian regimes: the first (incidentally communist) being beyond the pale but the second (incidentally right wing) fit associates for the United States. South Africa has felt less isolated and has acquired a firmer friend in the five-power Contact Group which has been trying to mediate between South Africa and Swapo and devise an agreement covering a cease-fire in Namibia, election procedures and constitutional safeguards. South Africa had been loath to abort this process but the advent of Reagan, by altering the tone in the Contact Group, gave Pretoria greater latitude for obstructiveness and delay – and also encouraged Pretoria to quicken its military operations in Namibia and in southern Angola where 30,000 South African troops and special units were employed to destroy Swapo bases and subvert the regime in Luanda. South Africa also launched limited military operations against Mozambique at the beginning of 1981 and into Lesotho at the end of 1982.

Finally, South African ambivalence has been conditioned by splits in the ruling Nationalist Party which were sharpened after Vorster was forced by half concealed scandals to resign the premiership in 1978. His successor, P. W. Botha, gave an appearance of flexibility and introduced constitutional proposals, but these have been more alarming to whites than convincing to blacks. Botha is opposed on his right not only by the Herstigte National Party but also by a new (1982) Conservative Party, a breakaway from the Nationalist Party led by its principal personality in its Transvaal heartland, Andreas Treurnicht, and by Connie Mulder, Vorster's presumptive successor before the scandals of 1978. With his position, and his resolve, thus weakened, Botha may well hesitate to couple domestic constitutional experiment with a retreat from Namibia. In sum: South Africa's impact on southern Africa remains paramount but its direction is uncertain both in the sense of undiscernible and in the sense of unsettled.

With both superpowers holding back the dominant foreign element in southern Africa is the presence of the Cubans who, having gone to Angola as friends of Agostinho Neto, have stayed there to sustain his successors against the combined threats from South Africa and Unita and are now Soviet mercenaries. To some extent they have been replaced by East Germans and other east Europeans. East Germany has a military contingent of 2,000–3,000 as well as specialists in training police, secret police and guerrillas. President Erich Honecker and his minister of defence, Heinz Hoffman, visited Angola (and other parts of southern Africa) in 1978 and Hoffman's deputy Helmuth Poppe supervised the invasion of Zaire's province of Shaba from Angola in that year. But in geopolitical terms a switch from

Cubans to East Germans is inconsequential.

These activities indicate a Soviet determination to hold on to its beachhead in southern Africa, if only vicariously and for the time being. Of a more purposeful or aggressive policy there have been few signs although a singularly impressive group of Soviet generals was spotted spying out the land in southern Angola in 1977. The group comprised no fewer than eleven generals, among them General V. I. Petrov, at that date the first deputy to the C-in-C of the Ground Forces of the Soviet Union and the key figure in the salvation of Mengistu from the Somali offensive. His companions in Angola included specialists in supply, air transport, planning, and electronic and radio intelligence. Petrov returned to Angola in the next year and also visited Mozambique.

In spite of this high-powered reconnaissance Soviet policy has remained in low key. This could be ascribed to the absorbing demands of action in Ethiopia, but more probably it is determined by the differences between the two areas, northeastern and southwestern Africa. In the Horn Soviet action, although massive when it came, was delayed until the last moment beyond which the Mengistu regime would have been engulfed. Furthermore, the Horn's strategic significance (in relation to the Middle East and Indian Ocean) is incomparably more immediate than southern Africa's. The Soviet Union is under no compulsion to act in the latter and will do so only at the behest of opportunity as opposed to need.

Opportunity exists. The Western allies are in a dilemma, denouncing *apartheid* but patently unwilling to be nasty to white South Africa, reluctantly accepting that the black side is the way of the future but still boxed into the white corner for reasons of colour and finance. Yet it is difficult for Moscow to turn Western disadvantage to Russian profit. Moscow's position is essentially negative. In African eyes the Soviet Union's one virtue is that it is a card to play against the United States; the Soviet Union is not loved for itself and has done little or nothing for Africa. Soviet aid to liberation movements has been only enough to keep the pot boiling; in the Rhodesian conflict Moscow chose the wrong pot; and neither in Rhodesia nor Namibia has Moscow risked becoming entangled in a major confrontation with South Africa. The Soviet Union shows no inclination to challenge the regional predominance of South Africa.

The United States are another reluctant giant. The 1970s were a testing time for them. They were forced to acknowledge defeat in Vietnam – a military retreat accompanied by pronounced symptoms of economic overstrain, by the demoralization of many in its armed forces, and by demonstrative protests at home against warmaking tactics which were excessively inhumane as well as fruitless. The defeat of a superpower is a phenomenon in itself and its effects are difficult to gauge. In the short term they were surprisingly slight. The regime remained intact and the reverse was absorbed, too distant to warrant extravagant or prolonged reaction. American society has proved remarkably resilient, partly thanks to its democratic elasticity and partly to an indifference to remote commotions.

But implicit in the defeat was the need to re-examine not only military tactics but also political strategy. The war in Vietnam had been presented in ideological terms. It was a war against Vietnamese communists or, alternatively or concurrently, a war to stop the spread of Chinese communism. As an ideology anti-communism has been in recent decades a more powerful emotion in the United States than communism is by now in the Soviet Union. Yet the victory of Vietnamese communism was accepted with considerable equanimity, and so it might be supposed that the American outlook on the world is becoming less ideological. Contrariwise the election of Ronald Reagan to the presidency pointed the other way.

The reverse in Vietnam might also be expected to blunt the American appetite for foreign adventures, at least temporarily. But this is too loose an assumption. While the American people and Congress may for a time sheer away from contests with adversaries like Ho Chih Minh there is no reason to conclude that they will hesitate to stand up to Soviet advances or pretensions anywhere in the world. American reluctance to become engaged in southern Africa is the corollary, not of a general unadventurousness, but of Moscow's comparatively restrained or incompetent performance in the area; and this proposition finds support in the fact that Washington's one clear and serious purpose in southern Africa has been the removal of the Cubans, the representatives of Soviet power and opportunity. Washington's concern is to assess how far the successes of Machel, Neto, Mugabe, Nujoma – or Didier Ratsirake in Mauritius in 1975, or Ali Soilih in the Comoros that same year (but murdered in 1978), or France-René Albert in the Seychelles in 1977 – are effectively successes for the Soviet Union too; and if they are, whether it is expedient to use open or covert violence against them.

In Angola, as in Morocco and the Horn, Americans haver uneasily between regional and global strategies. American insistence on linking a Cuban retreat with Namibian independence – applying global considerations to a regional conflict – not only delays a Namibian settlement but also commits Washington to the support of Angola's internal and external enemies (Unita and South Africa), obstructs the rapprochement for which Angola seems half prepared and validates Angolan dependence on the Soviet Union. Yet, given the nature of the South African regime on the one hand and on the other the Liberal traditions of the United States and its ethnic make-up, American support for Pretoria can never escape ambivalence. There is a gaping flaw in President Reagan's ideological and strategic bias towards South Africa and in the final analysis Washington has in southern Africa no policy which it can carry through.

There is therefore an air of unreality about the politics of southern Africa. There is conflict between black and white and the makings of conflict between the superpowers but the first conflict is very unevenly balanced and the second is vicarious, suspended and – more than anywhere else in the world – governed in both capitals by more irresolution than settled purpose. There is no other theatre of conflict where great events are more susceptible of being precipitated by accident.

NOTE: The peculiar offence of *apartheid* is not the base desire of the whites to be ruled by none except whites: that is an intelligible attitude which, in reverse, lay at the root of anti-colonialism. *Apartheid* is odious because, first, it equates inferiority with an irremoveable natural quality (pigmentation) and because, secondly, it persists in the goal of white supremacy even in circumstances which make the attainment of that goal impossible without evil means (such as torture).

8 IN CONCLUSION

I

Liberated Africa is undergoing changes, the like of which have never been experienced before.

They are not the changes that were envisaged at liberation. They are more profound, more abrupt and so far from being liberating they are shattering. They are superficially similar to changes with which other countries are having to cope in the twentieth century, but in that comparison lies a crucial difference. The twentieth century, now rolling over Africa, has not been fashioned by it. Elsewhere modern times, however disruptive, emerge from their own surroundings and their own past, whereas for Africans they do not. A culture, like a population, can take so much and no more. In material terms a population rejects growth of more than, say, 5 to 6 per cent a year because it cannot expand its essential services (sewage, for instance) at that speed. Analogously there is a limit to the changes which a culture can absorb if it is to remain sane and healthy.

Take, for example, the modern city. The modern city is far from being the monstrous cancer of some popular myths. It is nevertheless for many of its inhabitants ugly, noisy, dirty and cruel. But where it is a native product it is to that extent comparatively intelligible and endurable. Translated into a different culture it is dismayingly out of place and destructive. A city like Lagos (or Jakarta or Teheran) is in fact more acceptable to an American or European than it is to millions of the people who have to live in it.

Indigestible cultural change produces rejection symptoms. It turns people into refugees seeking comfort in a more familiar past. Where the brightness of the future proves illusory, even a dark past has its attractions. But they too can be unhealthy. One common manifestation is a revival of cults – comforting to the bewildered, curious to the anthropologists – which are at best irrational and at worst repulsive: a flight from reality into an emotional mirage and intellectual fog characteristic of times of trouble and transition in many ages and places. So behind the conflicts of tribe against tribe, Christian against Muslim, traditional chief and new urban boss, civilians and the military, there lies a latent struggle for leadership and allegiance between old priests and new mandarins. The mundane problems discussed in this book are tossed about on a vastly unruly scene upon which the outside observer should tread and comment only with humility and a generous spirit.

II

That said, there are nevertheless two strictures which should be pronounced without equivocation. The first concerns Africa's prodigal population increases, the second corruption.

Populations which double in not much more than a generation are unmanageable and unfeedable. The present demographic trend in Africa assumes – as much of the rest of the world assumes – that people can go on being fed with imported food. This is not merely a very dubious economic proposition, involving highly optimistic assumptions about the balance of payments – about, that is to say, the importing country's ability to pay for such imports. It is also, and equally dubiously, a physical proposition which, upon being brought down to specifics, holds that the United States will go on indefinitely producing exportable surpluses of food to be sold or given away to foreigners. There is no reason to suppose that this proposition is true and there are many reasons for supposing that it will be proved false no later than the end of this century. The stabilization of African populations is therefore a paramount requirement for good health and political order, to stave off certain misery and possible revolution; and in this context birth control does not mean a stop to procreation after the sixth or seventh child. It means that two are enough.

Secondly, corruption. Whether corruption flourishes more lushly in Africa than elsewhere is a futile question. Suffice it to say that it does flourish excessively. Corruption is morally odious, socially disruptive, economically expensive (even crippling), and politically tenacious. Its chief sources are greed, opportunity and emulation; its enemies are social stigma, punishment and stability, and the greatest of these three may well be the last. The man in power with the chance to make a bit on the side is doubly tempted if he believes that his power may not last and, once lost, will not be recovered. In a settled polity the politician who loses office expects to get it back one day: he has his ups and downs and lives with the latter in expectation of the former. But in an unsettled state the politician is in constant fear of being out of office for good and probably in gaol with his property and even his life at risk. So it seems to him sensible and prudent to get rich quick by hook or by crook and stash the proceeds away in a safely remote account. He will not stop treating office in this way until he can take a longer view of his career.

There is no short cut to this state of affairs. African societies, if they are to grow economically, will have to go through the same slow processes as Western Europe in the eighteenth and nineteenth centuries when corruption was reduced and the productive use of wealth was boosted by the realization that a position could be held and recovered – and wealth could be got and retained – over a lifetime. This attitude was a powerful aid to individual honesty.

III

But corruption is only a part of a larger problem.

Morality apart, the essence of the complaint against corruption is that moneys advanced as loans or gifts for particular purposes are not used for the purposes specified. But there are reasons besides corruption why this happens. International aid is not simply an extension of distributive economics. It is different in kind from the redistribution of wealth practised, or preached, within national societies. Such societies possess common and perceived rules and assumptions, whether they are honoured in the observance or in the breach. This is not true internationally, because the so-called international society is not a society except in the loosest sense: it is an agglomeration without cultural unity. In practice therefore donors from one culture give or lend upon assumptions which are invalid and they end up disappointed by failures which, from within their own cultures, they never anticipated or discounted and do not fully understand. An important example of such misunderstanding is provided by differing ideas about what money is for and what to do with it when you have it.

Donors come overwhelmingly from the cultural zone created by the nation states of Western Europe from the end of the Middle Ages onwards. Theirs has been one of the world's great success stories. It has had a number of ingredients, including temperate climate and chance and a vigorous intellectual tradition comparatively uncluttered by religion. But one other cultural factor played an indisputably major role: the thrift which characterized the increasingly powerful middle class of successful merchants, industrialists and bankers who became the dominant economic element in these societies. Thrift entails a belief in the value – the material value – of saving for the future. It both advertises and secures the benefits of taking the long view and, by a complex interaction of habit and calculation, lays up the capital necessary for economic expansion. Saving is the alternative to spending and, when successful, creates a climate hostile to the ostentatious spree. Saving is not morally superior to spending but it is economically much more constructive.

The values of the counting house as opposed to those of the bazaar underlie the modern history of Western Europe and North America. They are by no means wholly attractive – defective in generosity and contented with a singularly harsh method of measuring what is fair between man and man – but they have been strikingly effective and it is difficult to think of an alternative set of coherent values which is both more attractive and more successful. They have helped to confirm civilian rule as opposed to military, to abate corruption and to buttress stability. Their processes are arcane and it is impossible to predict whether, or at what pace, they may permeate the new states of Africa where they are at present conspicuously absent. But their absence doubly alienates their cultural opposites in the developed world who condemn a fecklessness which, in their eyes, is not only reprehensible but also a fatal bar to any steady economic development worthy of support.

And Africa must court this support. Any belief that Africa can pull itself up by its own bootstraps is, however morally admirable, an arithmetical absurdity. In their hearts most Africans know this but soliciting aid often goes against the grain. The need nevertheless is paramount if peoples are to be fed, find work and progress even modestly in mind and body, and this need is not diminished by the cases in which aid has been offered selfishly or even fraudulently: there have been as many honest and honourable instances. Acknowledging the need implies a lack of independence but need not entail a loss of pride, while rejecting aid is a disservice to countless Africans and a refusal to face facts. The problem is to devise terms that are fair and profitable to both sides (an issue on which Africans may well need a special kind of preliminary aid – objective professional advice in, for example, drawing up contracts) and to give donors better cause than they have had for supposing that aid will be used properly and fruitfully.

Aid for the Third World, including Africa, has been something of a charge on the conscience of the developed countries but not much of a charge on its purse. The case for aid is grounded in both altruism and self-interest. The case for altruism needs no elaboration. It is a moral imperative of blinding simplicity. But the practice of altruism is another matter. Non-Africans with – by world standards – money and goods to spare feel little compulsion to offer them to Africa on any but the strictest commercial terms. Charity not only begins at home; it ends there. Few countries do much for their own poor, let alone the foreign poor, and economic recession pushes generosity still further into the background. The record of aid to poor countries, whether given directly or through international bodies, is dismal. Even the richest countries cannot be persuaded to disburse 1 per cent of their GNP (the United States and Switzerland have managed 0.2 per cent, Britain 0.4 per cent and even the most generous – Sweden, Norway, France, the Netherlands – not quite 1 per cent).

Aid is not synonymous with gifts. There are many ways of helping the poor without reviving at the international level the ethos of the soup kitchen. All aid involves some sacrifice by the donor and it is wrong to pretend that aid is ever equally beneficial to donor and recipient. There are, however, non-charitable factors: two in particular.

The first is the political significance of a black community in the United States which, even if it gives African problems little thought most of the time, will allow them some and, in conjunction with the growing hispanic-American population, will from time to time direct American attention to the needs of these two large blocks of necessitous states, African and Latin American. The United States, rich in itself and a controlling influence in international bodies like the World Bank and the IMF, is the last country in the world capable of turning a completely deaf ear to the poor of the Third World.

Second, Africa is a market for the manufactured goods of all industrial countries. How good a market depends on its prosperity. The failures of the 1970s have made it appear a poor prospect but, as the Brandt Report emphasized (perhaps over-emphasized), the market is there and is needed by industrial countries competing ever more frenetically with each other for export sales. They have a stake in Africa's economic health – not a stake that will be enhanced by extravagant or indiscriminate lending but one that can be fortified by well-considered aid designed to turn latent economic demand into actuality. It is no good expecting industrialized states to help with the creation of industries in Africa which will increase unemployment in Europe and North America, but the development of communications, education and training, and agriculture is potentially valuable to the industrial world. This is a case where economic calculation interacts with incalculable expectations. So long as Africa looks like a disaster area aid will be meagre: to him that hath not, will not be given. But even small signs of improvement may radically alter the mood. A modest injection of capital may produce a large injection of hope, which in turn will justify the capital investment and add to it. Africa is dense with consumers who are the ultimate motor of economic expansion. Even in the recession of the late 1970s and early 1980s the Third World was taking a quarter or more of the exports of the industrialized countries and these – if IMF and other calculations are to be believed – have to look to the Third World for as much as half of their projected export growth.

Africa no longer relies solely on the industrialized world represented by the OECD. Its economic troubles in the 1970s were magnified by the rise in oil prices which enriched the members of OPEC at their expense and created, so Africans may argue, a counter-claim on OPEC's profits and generosity. OPEC countries have responded (their aid in 1980 approached 1.5 per cent of their combined GNP) but the total value of OPEC aid remains substantially below the total of OECD aid and has in addition been directed disproportionately to a few Muslim countries. Now and for some time to come significant foreign aid means OECD aid: North American, West European and Japanese.

The most successful modern example of economic aid across frontiers is the Marshall Plan. The Plan had important features which are absent from the African case: a single donor and, among the recipients, high levels of technical education, administrative competence and an efficient (if damaged) economic infrastructure. But the Marshall Plan had also one feature worth copying. The donor provided aid to a group of countries on the basis that the members of the group would themselves determine its allocation and application: it put therefore a premium on regional cooperation. The Americans did not purport to run Eruopean economies for Europeans; they provided the wherewithal and placed subsequent decisions in the collective hands of the beneficiaries. This pattern is applicable in Africa. SADCC, for example, is already seeking foreign funds for regional schemes and getting them. Success by SADCC will promote regional cooperation in other areas. It will also promote political stability within the several states of the group.

Political stability, which embraces demographic stability, is a prerequisite of economic aid. No stability, no aid: this is a virtually axiomatic proposition. But so is another: no aid, no stability. This is a chicken-and-egg situation. The debate whether to begin with the chicken or the egg is barren. So is waiting for either a chicken or an egg to materialize.

The affairs of most African states a generation after independence are not just stagnant, chaotic and disillusioning. The stagnation, chaos and disillusion have brought them to a point of precariousness which, given the circumstances of the world into which they have been born, have international repercussions of two kinds: these affairs cannot now be mended without outside help and it is unwise of outsiders not to help. But the outsiders do not wish to acknowledge the extent of their practical interest in the stability of the continent. So they pay more attention to its manifest failures than to its equally manifest needs, in which myopia they are abetted by African mismanagement (or worse) which serves as a moral and political alibi. This pattern of thought has been hardening over the decades and particularly in the last decade of global economic stringency. It is a pattern not only ungenerous but imprudent, for it progressively magnifies miseries, which may be localized, and turmoil, which may not.

APPENDICES

A. Area, population and date of independence
B. Domestic product
C. External trade and public debt
D. The Charter of the Organization for African Unity

APPENDIX A. AREA, POPULATION AND DATE OF INDEPENDENCE

	Area (000 sq. km)	*Total (millions)*	*Density (per sq. km)*	*Annual growth (per cent)*	*Date of independence*
		Population			
Algeria	2,382	20.3	9	3.5	1962
Angola	6247	7.4	6	2.6	1975
Benin	113	3.7	33	3.1	1960
Botswana	582	0.9	1.5	3.2	1966
Burundi	28	4.5	161	2.6	1962
Cameroon	475	8.9	19	2.5	1960
Cape Verde	4	0.3	75	1.6	1974
Central African Republic	623	2.4	4	2.4	1960
Chad	1,284	4.6	4	2.1	1960
Comoros	2	0.4	200	2.9	1975
Congo	342	1.6	5	2.7	1960
Djibuti	22	0.3	14	2.7	1977
Egypt	1,001	44.1	44	2.4	1922
Equatorial Guinea	28	0.4	14	2.5	1968
Ethiopia	1,224	32.9	27	2.5	1941
Gabon	268	0.6	2	1.5	1960
Gambia	4	0.6	150	2.6	1965
Ghana	92	12.5	136	3.3	1957
Guinea	246	5.3	22	2.7	1950
Guinea-Bissau	36	0.6	17	1.8	1974
Ivory Coast	322	8.6	27	3.2	1960
Kenya	580	17.9	31	4.1	1963
Lesotho	30	1.4	47	2.5	1966
Liberia	98	2.1	21	3.6	1847
Libya	1,775	3.2	2	3.8	1951
Madagascar	587	9.2	16	2.8	1960
Malawi	118	6.6	56	3.4	1964
Mali	1,240	7.3	6	2.8	1960
Mauritania	1,030	1.7	1.5	2.9	1960
Mauritius	2	0.9	485	1.6	1968
Morocco	459	21.7	47	3.2	1956
Mozambique	799	11.0	14	2.7	1975
Namibia	824	1.3	1.5	—	—
Niger	1,267	5.6	4	3.0	1960
Nigeria	924	82.4	89	3.4	1960
Rwanda	26	5.1	196	3.7	1962

APPENDIX A (*cont.*)

			Population		
	Area (9000 sq. km)	*Total (millions)*	*Density (per sq. km)*	*Annual growth (per cent)*	*Date of independence*
S Tome/Principe	1	0.1	100	—	1975
Senegal	196	6.0	31	2.7	1960
Seychelles	0.4	0.06	150	—	1976
Sierra Leone	72	3.7	51	2.8	1961
Somalia	638	5.1	8	3.7	1960
South Africa	1,134	31.0	27	2.9	1934
Sudan	2,506	19.4	8	2.9	1956
Swaziland	17	0.6	35	3.0	1968
Tanzania	945	19.1	20	3.2	1961
Togo	57	2.8	49	3.1	1960
Tunisia	164	6.7	41	2.4	1956
Uganda	241	14.1	58	3.2	1952
Upper Volta	274	7.3	27	2.7	1960
Zaire	2,345	29.9	13	2.9	1960
Zambia	753	6.2	8	3.3	1964
Zimbabwe	391	7.9	20	3.5	1980

Sources: UN Department of International Economic and Social Affairs
The Europa Year Book 1983 (Europa Publications. 1983).

APPENDIX B. DOMESTIC PRODUCT

	Gross ($ million)	*Per head ($)*
Algeria	19,738	1,102
Angola	2,701	432
Benin*	604	184
Botswana*	396	557
Burundi†	624	146
Cameroon	3,066	407
Cape Verde	.36	132
Central African Republic	391	179
Chad	693	172
Comoros	70	229
Congo	784	581
Djibuti*	90	809
Egypt*	18,775	485

	Gross ($ million)	*Per head ($)*
Equatorial Guinea	112	349
Ethiopia	2,669	97
Gabon†	2,660	4,926
Gambia★	95	172
Ghana	4,594	465
Guinea	723	164
Guinea-Bissau	177	335
Ivory Coast†	7,714	1,014
Kenya†	5,503	370
Lesotho	143	121
Liberia†	744	427
Libya†	19,971	7,262
Madagascar†	2,095	253
Malawi†	1,011	175
Mali	507	87
Mauritania†	544	353
Mauritius	769	873
Morocco†	12,426	654
Mozambique	2,722	296
Niger	736	160
Nigeria★	50,170	717
Rwanda★	771	176
Senegal★	1,958	373
Seychelles★	63	1,052
Sierra Leone★	711	221
Somalia	492	155
South Africa†	45,663	1,594
Sudan	5,310	338
Swaziland★	356	699
Tanzania†	4,354	263
Tunisia	5,964	988
Uganda	2,563	227
Upper Volta†	826	126
Zaire★	4,520	172
Zambia†	2,808	513
Zimbabwe	4,084	589

★　Estimate for 1977
†　Estimate for 1978
Other estimates are for 1975. It is hardly necessary to point out that average
GDP per head tells nothing about the distribution of the GDP. High *per caput*
wealth can co-exist with poverty.
Source: Yearbook of National Accounts Statistics 1979 (United Nations, 1980).

APPENDIX C. EXTERNAL TRADE AND PUBLIC DEBT

	Exports of goods (value) as % of imports	External debt at end of 1980 ($ million)	Debt service as % of exports	IDA Development Credits: total at mid-1982 ($ million)
Algeria	73	23,061.6	24.9	—
Angola	196	n.a.	n.a.	n.a.
Benin	10	718.7	n.a.	136.4
Botswana	n.a.	270.4	1.6	15.5
Burundi	69	292.3	n,a.	156.8
Cameroon	88	2,609.7	7.7	246.3
Central African Republic	127	211.3	4.5	56.9
Chad	50	231.2	n.a.	57.3
Comoros	49	95.2	n.a.	22.1
Congo	53	1,086.8	9.4	73.1
Egypt	48	17,385.7	18.9	945.2
Ethiopia	75	1,061.5	7.6	434.3
Gabon	222	1,552.3	17.5	—
Gambia	41	218.3	0.3	35.3
Ghana	69	1,306.4	6.0	203.9
Guinea	n.a.	1,747.7	n.a.	122.7
Ivory Coast	101	5,469.5	18.3	7.5
Kenya	67	3,058.6	9.5	506.4
Lesotho	n.a.	193.7	n.a.	69.6
Liberia	109	743.0	n.a.	71.7
Libya	215	—	—	—
Madagascar	88	1,552.0	7.3	310.4
Malawi	58	804.8	18.4	260.6
Mali	47	852.6	3.6	212.2
Mauritania	57	1,361.7	11.4	71.0
Mauritius	65	475.7	5.6	20.4
Morocco	49	9,155.6	27.6	51.6
Mozambique	46	n.a.	n.a.	n.a.
Niger	105	825.9	n.a.	181.7
Nigeria	77	7,147.8	1.9	36.9
Rwanda	39	272.3	1.1	168.0
Senegal	82	1,530.9	n.a.	244.9
Seychelles	24	42.3	0.4	—
Sierra Leone	58	402.3	15.5	65.2
Somalia	44	1,093.8	2.8	170.9
South African Customs Union	118	—	—	—

	Exports of goods (value) as % of imports	External debt at end of 1980 ($ million)	Debt service as % of exports	IDA Development Credits: total at mid-1982 ($ million)
Sudan	49	4,951.4	11.6	615.8
Swaziland	n.a.	230.9	3.1	8.0
Tanzania	41	2,258.3	8.9	691.5
Togo	54	1,026.5	n.a.	111.3
Tunisia	62	4,607.1	12.2	68.3
Uganda	315	954.9	12.8	235.7
Upper Volta	22	508.0	n.a.	222.6
Zaire	159	4,923.9	n.a.	399.4
Zambia	137	2,631.9	22.9	86.1
Zimbabwe	n.a.	749.3	2.6	13.2

Trade figures are for 1978 or 1979 except Angola (1974). Chad and Niger (1976) and Comoros, Ghana, Mozambique, Senegal and Uganda (1977).
Sources: 1979 Yearbook of International Trade Statistics (United Nations, 1980), *The World Bank Annual Report* 1982.

European aid via the EEC is a significant element in African trade and development. The first Yaounde Convention of 1964 with eighteen former French colonies was extended in 1969 to embrace the three former British territories in East Africa and followed by the wider Yaounde II covering 1971–75. Under the succeeding Lome Conventions the EEC programme included Caribbean and Pacific as well as African states. Grants and loans were supplemented by two special schemes: (i) STABEX, a stabilization fund to compensate producers of agricultural products and iron ores for loss of export earnings due to price fluctuations and (ii) SYSMIN, a similar fund for other minerals.

Africans and others complain that the Lome programmes were so enmeshed in bureaucratic procedures that the funds available, although substantial, remained largely undisbursed.

	Period	Number of ACP states	Total funds (m. ecu's)	STABEX	SYSMIN	Percentage undisbursed at the end of 1983
Lome I	1976–80	46	3390	375	—	35
Lome II	1981–85	61	5227	550	280	90

In 1980 over 40 per cent ACP exports were going to the EEC but the ACP share of EEC trade was only 7 per cent

APPENDIX D. THE CHARTER OF THE ORGANIZATION FOR AFRICAN UNITY IN FORCE FROM 13 SEPTEMBER 1963

We, the Heads of African and Malagasy States and Governments assembled in the City of Addis Ababa, Ethiopia;

CONVINCED that it is the inalienable right of all people to control their own destiny;

CONSCIOUS of the fact that freedom, equality, justice and dignity are essential objectives for the achievement of the legitimate aspirations of African peoples;

CONSCIOUS of our responsibility to harness the natural and human resources of our continent for the total advancement of our peoples in spheres of human endeavour;

INSPIRED by a common determination to promote understanding among our peoples and cooperation among our States in response to the aspirations of our peoples for brotherhood and solidarity, in a larger unity transcending ethnic and national differences;

CONVINCED that, in order to translate this determination into a dynamic force in the cause of human progress, conditions for peace and security must be established and maintained;

DETERMINED to safeguard and consolidate the hard-won independence as well as the sovereignty and territorial integrity of our States, and to resist neo-colonialism in all its forms;

DEDICATED to the general progress of Africa;

PERSUADED that the Charter of the United Nations and the Universal Declaration of Human Rights, to the principles of which we reaffirm our adherence, provide a solid foundation for peaceful and positive cooperation among states;

DESIROUS that all African States should henceforth unite so that the welfare and well-being of their peoples can be assured;

RESOLVED to reinforce the links between our States by establishing and strengthening commo institutions;

HAVE agreed to the present Charter.

Establishment

ARTICLE I

1. The High Contracting Parties do by the present Charter establish an Organization to be known as the 'Organization of African Unity'.

2. The Organization shall include the Continental African States, Madagascar and other Islands surrounding Africa.

Purposes

ARTICLE II

1. The Organization shall have the following purposes:

Independent Africa and the World

(a) To promote the unity and solidarity of the African States;
(b) To co-ordinate and intensify their collaboration and efforts to achieve a better life for the peoples of Africa;
(c) To defend their sovereignty, their territorial integrity and independence;
(d) To eradicate all forms of colonialism from Africa; and;
(e) To promote international cooperation, having due regard to the Charter of the United Nations and the Universal Declaration of Human Rights.

2. To these ends, the Member States shall coordinate and harmonize their general policies, especially in the following fields:

(a) Political and diplomatic cooperation;
(b) Economic cooperation, including transport and communications;
(c) Educational and cultural cooperation;
(d) Health, sanitation, and nutritional cooperation;
(e) Scientific and technical cooperation; and
(f) Cooperation for defence and security.

Principles
ARTICLE III
The Member States, in pursuit of the purposes stated in Article II, solemnly affirm and declare their adherence to the following principles:

1. The sovereign equality of all Member States;
2. Non-interference in the internal affairs of States;
3. Respect for the sovereignty and territorial integrity of each State and for its inalienable right to independent existence;
4. Peaceful settlement of disputes by negotiation, mediation, conciliation or arbitration;
5. Unreserved condemnation, in all its forms, of political assassination as well as of subversive activities on the part of neighbouring States or any other State;
6. Absolute dedication to the total emancipation of the African territories which are still dependent;
7. Affirmation of a policy of non-alignment with regard to all blocs.

Membership
ARTICLE IV
Each independent sovereign African State shall be entitled to become a Member of the Organization.

Rights and Duties of Member States
ARTICLE V
All Member States shall enjoy equal rights and shall have equal duties.

Institutions
ARTICLE VII
The Organization shall accomplish its purposes through the following principal institutions:

1. The Assembly of Heads of State and Government;

2. The Council of Ministers;
3. The General Secretariat;
4. The Commission of Mediation, Conciliation and Arbitration.

The Assembly of Heads of State and Government
ARTICLE VIII
The Assembly of Heads of State and Government shall be the supreme organ of the Organization. It shall, subject to the provisions of this Charter, discuss matters of common concern to Africa with a view to coordinating and harmonizing the general policy of the Organization. It may in addition review the structure, functions and acts of all the organs and any specialized agencies which may be created in accordance with the present Charter.

ARTICLE IX
The Assembly shall be composed of the Heads of State and Government or their duly accredited representatives and it shall meet at least once a year. At the request of any Member State and on approval by a two-thirds majority of the Member States, the Assembly shall meet in extraordinary session.

ARTICLE X
1. Each Member State shall have one vote.
2. All resolutions shall be determined by a two-thirds majority of the Members of the Organization.
3. Questions of procedure shall require a simple majority. Whether or not a question is one of procedure shall be determined by a simple majority of all Member States of the Organization.
4. Two-thirds of the total membership of the Organization shall form a quorum at any meeting of the Assembly.

ARTICLE XI
The Assembly shall have the power to determine its own rules of procedure.

The Council of Ministers
ARTICLE XII
1. The Council of Ministers shall consist of Foreign Ministers or such other ministers as are designated by the Governments of Member States.
2. The Council of Ministers shall meet at least twice a year. When requested by any Member State and approved by two-thirds of all Member States, it shall meet in extraordinary session.

ARTICLE XIII
1. The Council of Ministers shall be responsible to the Assembly of Heads of State and Government. It shall be entrusted with the responsibility of preparing conferences of the Assembly.
2. It shall take cognizance of any matter referred to it by the Assembly. It shall be entrusted with the implementation of the decisions of the Assembly of Heads of State and Government. It shall coordinate interAfrican cooperation

in accordance with the instructions of the Assembly and in conformity with article II (2) of the present Charter.

ARTICLE XIV
1. Each Member State shall have one vote.
2. All resolutions shall be determined by a simple majority of the members of the Council of Ministers.
3. Two-thirds of the total membership of the Council of Ministers shall form a quorum for any meeting of the Council.

ARTICLE XV
The Council shall have the power to determine its own rules of procedure.

General Secretariat
ARTICLE XVI
There shall be an Administrative Secretary-General of the Organization, who shall be appointed by the Assembly of Heads of State and Government. The Administrative Secretary-General shall direct the affairs of the Secretariat.

ARTICLE XVII
There shall be one or more Assistant Secretaries-General of the Organization, who shall be appointed by the Assembly of Heads of State and Government.

ARTICLE XVIII
The functions and conditions of services of the Secretary-General, of the Assistant Secretaries-General and other emiryees of the Secretariat shall be governed by the provisions of this Charter and the regulations approved by the Assembly of Heads of State and Government.
1. In the performance of their duties the Administrative Secretary-General and his staff shall not seek or receive instructions from any government or from any other authority external to the Organization. They shall refrain from any action which might reflect on their position as international officials responsible only to the Organization.
2. Each member of the Organization undertakes to respect the exclusive character of the responsibilities of the Administrative Secretary-General and the Staff and not seek to influence them in the discharge of their responsibilities.

Commission of Mediation. Conciliation, and Arbitration
ARTICLE XIX
Member States pledge to settle all disputes among themselves by peaceful means and, to this end, decide to establish a Commission of Mediation, Conciliation and Arbitration, the composition of which and conditions of service shall be defined by a separate Protocol to be approved by the Assembly of Heads of State and Government. Said Protocol shall be regarded as forming an integral part of the present Charter.

Specialized Commissions
ARTICLE XX
The Assembly shall establish such Specialized Commissions as it may deem necessary, including the following:
6. Economic and Social Commission;
2. Educational and Cultural Commission;
3. Health, Sanitation, and Nutrition Commission;
4. Defence Commission;
5. Scientific, Technical and Research Commission.

ARTICLE XXI
Each Specialized Commission referred to in Article XX shall be composed of the Ministers concerned or other Ministers or Plenipotentiaries designated by the Governments of the Member States.

ARTICLE XXII
The functions of the Specialized Commissions shall be carried out in accordance with the provisions of the present Charter and of the regulations approved by the Council of Ministers.

The Budget
ARTICLE XXIII
The budget of the Organization prepared by the Administrative Secretary-General shall be approved by the Council of Ministers. The budget shall be provided by contributions from Member States in accordance with the scale of assessment of the United Nations; provided, however, that no Member State shall be assessed an amount exceeding twenty per cent of the yearly regular budget of the Organization. The Member States agree to pay their respective contributions regularly.

Signature and Ratification of Charter
ARTICLE XXIV
1. The Charter shall be open for signature to all independent sovereign African States and shall be ratified by the signatory States in accordance with their respective constitutional processes.
2. The original instrument, done if possible in African languages, in English and French, all texts being equally authentic, shall be deposited with the Government of Ethiopia which shall transmit certified copies thereof to all independent sovereign African States.
3. Instruments of ratification shall be deposited with the Government of Ethiopia, which shall notify all signatories of each such deposit.

Entry into Force
ARTICLE XXV
This Charter shall enter into force immediately upon receipt by the Government of Ethiopia of the instruments of ratification from two-thirds of the signatory States.

Registration of the Charter

ARTICLE XXVI

This Charter shall, after due ratification, be registered with the Secretariat of the United Nations through the Government of Ethiopia in conformity with Article 102 of the Charter of the United Nations.

Interpretation of the Charter

ARTICLE XXVII

Any question which may arise concerning the interpretation of this Charter shall be decided by a vote of two-thirds of the Assembly of Heads of State and Government, of the Organization.

Adhesion and Accession

ARTICLE XXVIII

1. Any independent sovereign African State may at any time notify the Administrative Secretary-General of its intention to adhere or accede to this Charter.
2. The Administrative Secretary-General shall, on receipt of such notification, communicate a copy of it to all the Member States. Admission shall be decided by a simple majority of the Member States. The decision of each Member State shall be transmitted to the administrative Secretary-General, who shall, upon receipt of the required number of votes, communicate the decision to the State concerned.

Miscellaneous

ARTICLE XXIX

The working languages of the Organization and all its institutions shall be, if possible African languages, English and French.

ARTICLE XXX

The Administrative Secretary-General may accept on behalf of the Organization gifts, bequests and other donations made to the Organization, provided that this is approved by the Council of Ministers.

ARTICLE XXXI

The Council of Ministers shall decide on the privileges and immunities to be accorded to the personnel of the Secretariat in the respective territories of the Member States.

Cessation of Membership

ARTICLE XXXII

Any State which desires to renounce its membership shall forward a written notification to the Administrative Secretary-General. At the end of one year from the date of such notification, if not withdrawn, the Charter shall cease to apply with respect to the renouncing State, which shall thereby cease to belong to the Organization.

Amendment to the Charter

ARTICLE XXXIII

This Charter may be amended or revised if any Member State makes a written request to the Administrative Secretary-General to that effect; provided, however, that the proposed amendement is not submitted to the Assembly for consideration until all the Member States have been duly notified of it and a period of one year has elapsed. Such an amendment shall not be effective unless approved by at least two-thirds of all the Member States.

IN FAITH WHEREOF, We the Heads of African State and Government, have signed this Charter.

MAPS

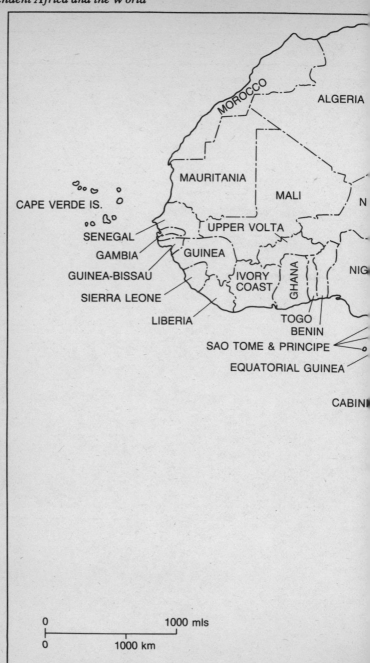

ALGERIA

MOROCCO

MAURITANIA

MALI

N

CAPE VERDE IS.

UPPER VOLTA

SENEGAL

GAMBIA

GUINEA

GUINEA-BISSAU

IVORY
COAST

GHANA

NIG

SIERRA LEONE

TOGO

LIBERIA

BENIN

SAO TOME & PRINCIPE

EQUATORIAL GUINEA

CABIN

0   1000 mls
0   1000 km

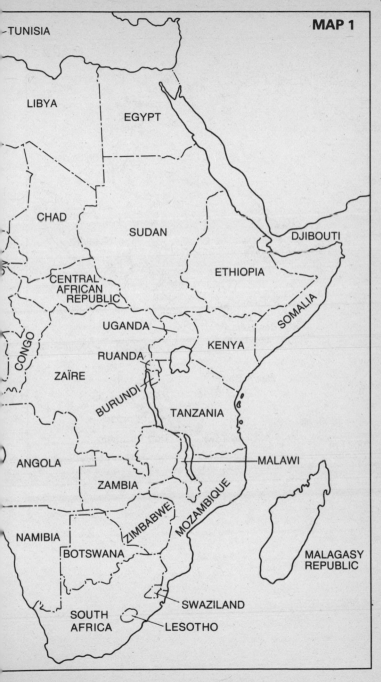

MAP 1

TUNISIA

LIBYA

EGYPT

CHAD

SUDAN

DJIBOUTI

CENTRAL
AFRICAN
REPUBLIC

ETHIOPIA

CONGO

UGANDA

SOMALIA

KENYA

RUANDA

ZAÏRE

BURUNDI

TANZANIA

ANGOLA

MALAWI

ZAMBIA

MOZAMBIQUE

NAMIBIA

ZIMBABWE

MALAGASY
REPUBLIC

BOTSWANA

SWAZILAND

SOUTH
AFRICA

LESOTHO

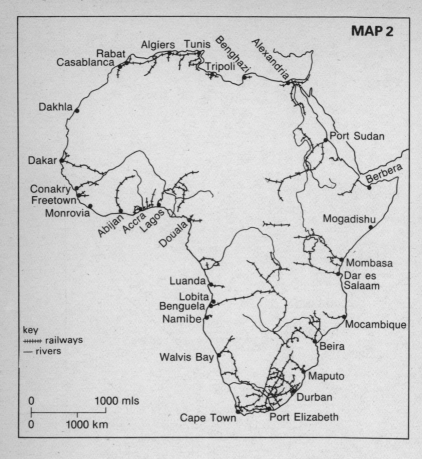

MAP 2

Algiers Tunis
Rabat
Casablanca
Benghazi
Alexandria
Tripoli

Dakhla

Port Sudan

Dakar

Berbera

Conakry
Freetown
Monrovia
Abijan Accra
Lagos
Douala

Mogadishu

Mombasa
Dar es
Salaam

Luanda

Lobita
Benguela
Namibe

Mocambique

Beira

Walvis Bay

Maputo

Durban

Cape Town   Port Elizabeth

key
╫╫╫ railways
— rivers

0   1000 mls
0   1000 km

INDEX

Abboud, Ibrahim, 74
Acheampong, General, 2
agriculture
  aid for, 33-8, 48, 95-6, 105
  cash crops, 36-7, 39, 42, 52, 64, 74, 95-6
  collective and communal, 47-8, 95-6
  colonial, 38
  droughts, 48, 51
  exports, 33, 36, 39, 52, 64, 74
  food, 50-2, 64
  neglected, 2, 20, 33-5, 39, 42, 50, 64
  Soviet, 52
aid, foreign, 2, 33-4, 119, 121-2
  for agriculture, 33-8, 48, 95-6, 105
  to Algeria, 101-2
  to Angola, 90, 105-16
  from Belgium, 83
  to Botswana, 105
  from Britain, 65, 121
  to Burundi, 102-3
  to Cameroon, 84
  to Central African Republic, 84
  to Chad, 84
  from China, 65, 101-5
  for communications development, 31-2, 65, 103-4
  to Congo, 98, 101-2
  to Congo-Brazzaville, 84, 103, 107
  from Cuba, 106-13
  from eastern Europe, 108, 113
  to Egypt, 73, 91
  to Ethiopia, 75, 77-9, 91
  from France, 36-7, 72, 80, 83-5, 121

to Gabon, 84
to Ghana, 42, 44, 94-7, 101, 106
to Guinea, 44-5, 94-7, 101, 105, 107
from IMF, 82
industrial, 33-4, 43-5, 61, 73, 95, 97
to Ivory Coast, 36-7
from Japan, 122
to Kenya, 38, 79
from Libya, 108
to Libya, 71
to Mali, 94, 97, 101-2, 105
military, 46, 71-2, 75-9, 83-4, 90-9
  passim, 106-10, 113
to Morocco, 72
to Mozambique, 112
from Nigeria, 109
to Nigeria, 91, 98-9
from OPEC, 122
from Saudi Arabia, 80, 83
to Sierra Leone, 107
to Somalia, 76-7, 80, 102
from South Africa, 112-13
to South Africa, 61
to South Yemen, 107
from Soviet Union, 44-5, 71-9, 83, 90-9, 108, 114-16, 121
to Tanzania, 46, 48, 103-4
technological, 33-4, 60, 95, 97, 106
from USA, 44, 77-9, 83, 91, 108, 115
from Zaire, 108
to Zaire, 82-3
to Zambia, 65, 104
to Zimbabwe, 90, 114
see also debt